A Moment, A Lifetime

Between Ignorance and Enlightenment (*III*)

By
Venerable Master Hsing Yun

Translated by
Venerable Miao Hsi & Cherry Lai

By Venerable Master Hsing Yun
Translated by Venerable Miao Hsi and Cherry Lai
Edited by Edmond Chang, Robin Stevens, and Brenda Bolinger
Book designed by Dung Trieu and Ching Tay
Cover designed by Chun-Er Cheng

Published by Buddha's Light Publishing
3456 South Glenmark Drive
Hacienda Heights, CA 91745
Phone: 626-923-5144; 626-961-9697 Fax: 626-923-5145
E-mail: info@blpusa.com Website: www.blpusa.com

ISBN 1-932293-18-3

Library of Congress Cataloging-in-Publication Data

Xingyun, da shi.
[Cha na bu li. English.]
A moment, a lifetime : between ignorance and enlightenment (III) / By Venerable Master Hsing Yun ; Translated by Venerable Miao Hsi & Cherry Lai.
p. cm.
ISBN 1-932293-18-3 (pbk. : alk. paper)
1. Buddhism--Doctrines. I. Title.

BQ4165.X5613 2006
294.3'444--dc22

2005031254

Contents

Foreword

Since the inauguration of the daily paper, the *Merit Times*, in Taiwan on April 1, 2001, I have been writing an article each day for the column "Between Ignorance and Enlightenment." It is now nearly two years and I am still writing.

In the beginning, I was only trying it out, thinking I would finish in a couple of months. However, response from readers has been very enthusiastic, and I just could not stop writing.

Among the feedback from our readers, the staff at the *Merit Times* reported that many people subscribed to the paper because they wanted to read "Between Ignorance and Enlightenment." Some readers also indicated that after reading the column, their interests and skills in writing had improved. They were even able to gain acceptance to a university with their polished writing skills. Other readers made scrapbooks of the articles and used them as bedtime reading.

In addition, after reading the column some people who previously had numerous unwholesome habits have changed for the better. For instance, they have quit smoking, drinking, and gambling. There were also cases where family members had problems getting along with each other and they were inspired by the articles. Their families have become harmonious and joyful, filled with laughter and warmth. Some students wrote reports based on the articles and obtained high grades and commendation from their teachers.

These responses from different walks of life greatly reinforced my sense of duty for the column. Because of this mission, which I feel I must shoulder myself, I am motivated to write each and every day.

Regardless of how busy my schedule in propagating the Dharma may be, I can always find time during the day to make connections with the readers through my writing.

The English section of the American edition of the *Merit Times* is also publishing the articles translated by Hsi Lai Temple. Many study groups organized by members of the Buddha's Light International Association are using the articles for their discussions. Numerous readers have since called for a collective publication of these articles, and their earnest requests are now fulfilled.

The meaning of "Between Ignorance and Enlightenment" is actually reflected in our everyday life where there are inevitably many situations involving both "ignorance" and "enlightenment." Sometimes, those directly affected are deluded, while those around them may see through the situation very clearly. Therefore, a few appropriate words will be of much help in pointing the way to a breakthrough, providing food for thought at the same time.

In reality, ignorance and enlightenment lie in just a thought! A thought of ignorance may cause sorrow and pain, while an inspiration of enlightenment can bring out the sun of wisdom. Just as Buddhist sutras indicate, "Troubles are bodhi, and bodhi is trouble!" The sourness of pineapples and grapes can be turned into sweetness with sunshine and warm breezes. Therefore, by being able to reflect and contemplate on the sourness of our ignorance, we can taste the sweetness of enlightenment right here and now.

This short publication is the third in a projected series of at least ten volumes. Through "Between Ignorance and Enlightenment," I wish to share and to grow with all my readers!

Hsing Yun

Preface

From Ignorance to Enlightenment is the whole span of samsara–the inexorable cycle of birth and death of every sentient being. Its beginning is beyond thought and speculation, said the Buddha. Accordingly, we are asked not to waste our energy and time in a futile effort to unravel the beginnings. In the telling parable of the wounded man, the Buddha's advice to us is to start from the known present, delve into the reality of impermanence and resulting suffering, recognize that one has to work for one's own liberation, and seek a remedy to redress every problem. This is exactly what the Venerable Grand Master Hsing Yun has done in his pithy and timely mini-discourses published in a regular column of the daily *Merit Times* since its inception.

This is the third collection of such mini-discourses to be published in book form. It is most appropriately called *A Moment, A Lifetime*. In Buddhist psychology as expounded in the *Abhidhamma*, a moment is a lifetime of a single thought. During this brief period of time, a thought arises, exists and dies, giving way to a new thought. From the moment an external stimulus disturbs the underlying subconscious of the bhavanga (the life-continuum), it takes seventeen sequential moments for a concept to be formed though a process of receiving, analyzing, identifying, determining, and registering data and taking action on them. In the same analysis of the thought process, the *Abhidhamma* speaks of seven moments of impulsion (javana) when wholesome and unwholesome karma are formed. In the Buddhist concept of time, a moment thus assumes infinite proportions, as a lifetime is but an accumulation of moments. Each such moment determines the sum total of the final success or otherwise of a life. A moment is truly a lifetime.

It is with such thoughts on the title that I began to read the eighty mini-discourses of this volume, commencing, of course, with the essay entitled "A Moment, A Lifetime." The message of the Grand Master was as I expected: "We should tell ourselves that anything we do, benefiting others is for a lifetime, and hard work is only for a moment....For the sake of this lifetime and the many lifetimes to come, we must pay careful attention to the effect a moment may have in anything we do."

Each mini-discourse is a concise and succinct essay, a story, or an insightful pronouncement on an urgent and pressing human experience or issue. Each is replete with admirable sagacity establishing a lesson to be learned and applied to real life. The practical wisdom couched in each item reflects first of all Grand Master's profound and ever-expanding erudition. Here is a self-made scholar, well-versed in the rich Buddhist tradition of scholarship extending to scriptures, commentaries and treatises of all traditions, schools, and sects. To him Buddhism is a seamless web where neither boundaries nor divisions interfere with access to insight into life's problems.

What matters to Venerable Grand Master Hsing Yun is not where an idea occurs or who has preserved it. What matters to him is the collective wisdom of twenty-six centuries of Buddhist experience in the continent of Asia and elsewhere. His interpretation of Humanistic Buddhism is therefore an irreproachable approach to distill the essence of the whole of Buddhist wisdom and values. Each mini-discourse also represents the unique experiences of a lifetime of unwavering dedication to human service under the most trying and equally rewarding circumstances. It is his own life that he holds before the reader as a tested example for inspiration and emulation. His own assessment of wisdom is worthy of note: "although wisdom is a combination of natural endowment and acquired learning, the latter carries much more weight than the former. Through hard work and effort, one can make up any deficiency."

As a devoted worker for human progress, who has made many an indelible footprint on the sands of time, his advice in the opening essay is: "There is no elevator in the world that can lift you up straight to the level of success. We must walk up the stairway and make a footprint with every step we take." He returns to this theme with his own delightful parable of the two mountain climbers who climbed to the eightieth floor to their apartment only to find that the key was left behind on the fortieth floor. In "The Stairway of Life": he draws from this the lesson: "By the time eighty is reached, we may reflect on the past–the key was left on the fortieth floor, but we no longer have the strength to go back for it to open the door to our happy home."

The gifted and accomplished storyteller the Grand Master is, he invents his own parables which are as expressive and meaningful as the ones he chooses from the extensive Buddhist literature and folklore. He is, no doubt, an avid and judicious reader and purveyor of traditional knowledge. What he covers includes history, biographies, and anecdotes on human behavior, progress, and the search for wisdom. He is equally at home whether he recounts the mysteries of Chan koans, the depths of Buddhist philosophy, or anecdotes of Chinese Emperors, Beethoven, Edmund Hillary, Abder Rahman III and so forth. He finds parallels for life issues in the traffic code and the organization of a hospital as much as in politics and science. A revelation of this significant skill of the Grand Master comes out in his discussion of DNA and karma.

"Stop, Look, and Listen" is inspired by a signpost at a railroad crossing. The point he makes on its application to life is poignant: "Stop, so that we can be prepared and have the strength to start over again. Listen, so that we know the responses and sentiments of those around us. Look, so that we are sure of where to go....The crossing of life may also be crisscrossed by different kinds of invincible forces: isn't it wise to stop, look, and listen each time you cross?" The very next essay takes its cue from a gas station to remind us that "On the path of life, we also need to refill every so often in order to reach our goals." "Life is like a highway," he notes in the next item. Applying the Highway Code to life he tells us: "Seasoned motorists know how to stay out of trouble with the authorities. They slow down at curves and when going under overpasses. And they watch out for highway troopers on exit lanes." Of course his metaphor does not end there. He proceeds to discuss speed limits, carpool lanes, and maintenance of vehicles, and concludes, "The way of life can be found within the concept of speed limits." He returns to the theme later and calls life a marathon with no end to everyone competing for his or her place.

One reads these mini-discourses with sheer delight for they are witty, wise, and cogent. The optimism which each exudes is extraordinary. "The future is better than the past," he asserts because "it is full of endless possibilities." As one gets the message, one is amused by the Grand Master's ingenious parable of the two dogs: the little dog who chases his own tail because a dog's happiness is in its tail and the big dog who walks straight for the same reason because happiness follows immediately behind when it walks forward with all its might. His optimistic and positive attitude to life is also expressed in such statements as the following: "Human nature is basically good. ...Deep within our mind is a civilized world" and "Most of us are upright and law-abiding. We are reasonable and do our best in our roles." So does he speak of all action taken for the benefit of humanity as "Projects of

Hope." He even stresses that "Impermanence is not completely pessimistic. Because of impermanence, where there was formerly nothing, something new can happen....Impermanence is truly wonderful. As the saying goes, 'The good will come when the bad leaves.'"

Buddhism in its rich diversity is the underlying inspiration for the Grand Master's writings. He penetrates deeply into the teachings of the Buddha, commentaries and interpretations of various masters, and the pervading wisdom of both precept and practice. He thereby finds illustrations from an unending array of Buddhist anecdotes whether it be the story of Kisa Gotami and the mustard seed (here in the version of a stalk of auspicious grass) or that of the beleaguered man hanging for his life on a vine which was constantly being gnawed by a black mouse and a white mouse.

His capacity to present the most abstruse philosophical argument in the most lucid language with convincing illustrations is best demonstrated by the manner in which each item highlights an intrinsic truism of the Buddha's teachings. Conclusions he draws are invariably baffling as, for example, his view on deities and the Buddha: "Deities and Buddha are different; not all of us can become deities, but each and everyone possesses the Buddha nature within ourselves and can become Buddhas."

I have read this book with the greatest pleasure and profit. It is a pleasure because every page is full of such interesting and illuminating information, ingenious argument, thought-provoking intellectual challenge, and remarkably enlightening insights. The profit comes from the reassurance that life is good and beautiful, problems have solutions, and wisdom guides one through a life of happiness. Not once did I encounter a moment of dullness as I read most earnestly not only this volume but also its two predecessors. It is with a profound sense of satisfaction that I invite readers to share the joy I experienced in walking with the Grand Master through "A Moment, A Lifetime."

Ananda W.P. Guruge
President of the World Buddhist University Council
Former Ambassador of Sri Lanka to UNESCO,
France and USA

Acknowledgments

We received a lot of help from many people and we want to thank them for their efforts in making the publication of this book possible. We especially appreciate Venerable Tzu Jung, the Chief Executive of Fo Guang Shan International Translation Center (F.G.S.I.T.C.), Venerable Hui Chi, the Abbot of Hsi Lai Temple, Venerable Yi Chao and Venerable Miao Hsi for their support and leadership; Venerable Miao Hsi and Cherry Lai for their translation. We want to thank Edmond Chang, Mu-Tzen Hsu, Pey-Rong Lee, Dung Trieu, Chun-Er Cheng, and Kevin Hsyeh for their efforts in preparing the second edition. Robin Stevens, Brenda Bolinger, Ching Tay, Mei-Chi Shih, Dr. Richard Kimball, Louvenia Ortega, James Baquet, Agnes Ho, Virginia Wong, Venerable Miao Han, and Echo Tsai worked tirelessly on the first edition. We hope that each new edition will both benefit and inspire the reader.

A Moment, A Lifetime

Between Ignorance and Enlightenment (*III*)

A Footprint with Every Step

"A footprint with every step" is a popular saying today. During political campaigns, candidates especially like to emphasize that they have arrived at where they are by making "a footprint with every step." They portray themselves as being down-to-earth and realistic, the type of people that rely on hard work. The phrase should actually relate to the legacy a person has left behind, which cannot be easily erased.

"A footprint with every step" is encouragement for those who have worked hard that their well-earned achievements will naturally be recognized by society. It is the record of the traces a person makes through his or her resilience and progress towards what is wholesome and beautiful. Therefore, making "a footprint with every step" is not something that an individual can claim on his or her own; rather, it should be verified by those who have witnessed it.

People often say, "Where there is a will, there is a way." In life, it is only through making a footprint with every step we take that we can create a way. In walking, we must give up the previous step before we can move ahead to take the next one. However, if we stop and refuse to lift our foot to move forward, how can we expect to have a future? It is only by letting go of our previous footing that we can make progress. As the saying goes, "We should not fear being slow; we should fear coming to a standstill." By being stubborn and conservative, many people fail to leave lasting footprints. How are they supposed to succeed?

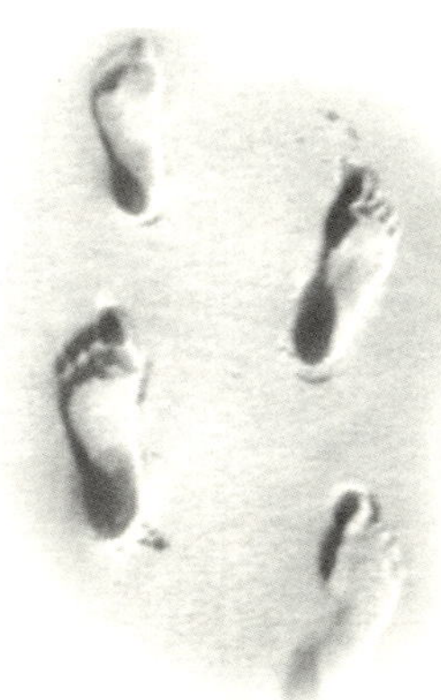

Some people like to say, "I've crossed more bridges than you've walked roads." On the long path of life, it is admirable to have come a long way, but we have to consider where we have left our footprints. Are they footprints in the mud, on the sand, amidst thorny bushes, on a rugged trail, or on a broad smooth road?

In making a footprint with every step,

some walk ahead with others behind following; some walk ahead with others behind watching; some walk ahead with others behind praising them; then some walk ahead with others behind criticizing and blaming them. For instance, in a family, children watch the footprints of their parents. In school, students look at those of their teachers. In an organization, subordinates check those of their supervisors. In a country, citizens observe those of politicians, scholars, and experts.

Wise readers, have you ever examined your own footprints? Do you have footprints of compassion, wisdom, humility, and gratitude? Are your footprints similar to those of the virtuous and the wise, both open and honest? There is no elevator in the world that can lift you up straight to the level of success. We must walk up the stairway and make a footprint with every step we take.

History is no more than the traces our ancestors have left us with every step they took, and which we now follow. In the future, we should also leave behind a path of our own that will guide the next generation, so that each successive generation will also make its own footprints with every step on the way to a bright future.

Know Ourselves

We all have two eyes with which to look at the world, to look at all matters, and to look at others, but we do not use them to look at ourselves. We all have a discriminating mind with which to discern others, matters, and the world, but we do not use it to discern ourselves.

We can see the faults of others, but not our own shortcomings. We can see the greed of others, but not our own stinginess. We can see the deviant views of others, but not our own ignorance. We can know the world and understand history. We can know our communities, friends, and relatives, but not know ourselves.

If we look at ourselves in the mirror, we can see the features of our face. We might be able to discern if we are good-looking or otherwise, but we cannot see our true mind. If there were a mirror that could reflect our mind, the greed, jealousy, selfishness, hatred, and grievances we might see would look really ugly indeed!

There are compassionate and vicious people; which are we? There are generous and greedy people; which are we? There are people who tolerate others and those who can only be tolerated; which are we? Then, there are people who sacrifice themselves for others and those who benefit at the expense of others; which are we?

As humans, we should be respectful, ethical, and humble. We should have trust, righteousness, and equality. We should have loyalty, filial piety, and benevolence. And we should be compassionate, generous, and joyful. In examining ourselves, do we possess all these qualities a person should have?

In fostering the strength to shoulder responsibility, we need to start from knowing and disciplining ourselves. We should be especially aware of our shortcomings and weaknesses. We must courageously face our faults in order to make smooth progress and grow accordingly.

In Buddhism, there is a well-known saying: "Know one's own original face." Do we really know our original face? So many of us are too busy calculating the gains and losses of others or blaming them for their lack of morals and knowledge. But, we forget to consider the arising and cessation of our own thoughts. It is indeed regrettable if we do not know our ideals, responsibilities, and missions in life, thus wasting our lives away without accomplishing anything.

The worst tragedy in the world is not knowing ourselves. Someone who does not know himself or herself is often deluded about reality and lacking in conscience, thus obstructing the development of his or her life of wisdom. In learning Buddhism, we learn to develop our own true mind, to remove the masks we wear, to honestly analyze ourselves, and to know ourselves.

Knowing ourselves is one of life's most important lessons. We should never take it lightly!

A Broad and Open Life

To live a broad and open life is to be open-minded and see through situations; however, we often cannot do so because we are bound by all kinds of afflictions. How can we be happy if we stay boxed up in a house without doors? If we lived in a castle, but could not leave for a long period of time, we would also consider the world to be small.

We love money and social status, so we can easily become bound by them. When we are trapped in selfish love, we become attached. When we love without freedom, when we love single-mindedly, when we are bound by love, it is all due to the lack of an open mind. When our lives are boxed in, it is like looking at the sky from the bottom of a well. There is no way we can appreciate the broadness of the open sky. As common folks, we can easily be bound by a person or affected by a few words of gossip. In fact, when we are enmeshed in gossip and lacking broad minds and open hearts, it is very difficult to live happily.

There are people who are attached to money and become enslaved by it; others cannot let go of material possessions and become imprisoned by them. Some people refuse to travel because they want to watch and protect their property. Others keep a pet and will not allow other dogs or cats in their homes. Some people waste much of life watching over the graves of their loved ones. Others plan and scheme just for the sake of securing a position. If we each have a broad and open life, a mind as vast as the universe, and thoughts as numerous as the sands of the Ganges River, how can we still be bound by such entanglements in the world?

Chan Master Jin Bifeng was too fond of his jade alms bowl, and because of his greedy attachment, he was almost captured by agents of death, who were sent to find him by the King of Hell. Fortunately, he was able to quickly awaken to this danger and ended up smashing his jade bowl, freeing himself from greed. At this point, he said, "If someone wants to capture Jin Bifeng, try binding space with chains; if space can be bound, then come and get Jin Bifeng." Being able to break through the attachment to his greed, he entered into a broad and open life.

Maitreya Bodhisattva once wrote, "Walking or sitting, I carry the bag. Putting it down, what carefree ease!" Maitreya Bodhisattva was not burdened by his bag, and Chan Master Jin Bifeng was ultimately not bound by his jade alms bowl. They were able to possess what they had and let go when they needed to.

When one is able to let go of everything, life becomes so free and easy. A broad and open life is so beautiful!

To Live Wisely

What is the best thing one can have in life? Some people wish to have a big house, a beautiful wife, and many children, while others dream of fancy cars, jewelry, stocks, and prime real estate. However, none of these are the most important possession; the most important gift we can have is wisdom.

Wisdom is the best guidance we can have in life. Facing adversity, we can use our wisdom to change the situation for the better, thus opening up a whole new world for ourselves. What is meant by "wisdom"? To gain understanding is only the beginning of wisdom, for knowledge is not the same as wisdom. We acquire knowledge through learning, but achieve wisdom through realization. True wisdom comes from constantly learning new things and applying that knowledge to our lives. It can be cultivated through hearing the teachings of the Buddha, contemplating their meaning, and practicing them in daily life.

Human civilization has made tremendous strides because of the collective wisdom of the human race, and not through wealth. Therefore, we should be most fearful of ignorance. Instead, developing the wisdom in our mind is fundamental to eradicating suffering. A wise person will never set foot on the wrong path because he or she knows and understands everything correctly.

To have wisdom is to have unlimited wealth. There is a limitation on how much a person can labor and work, but if we can cultivate our true inner resource, wisdom, our lives will be happy and fulfilled.

To have wisdom is to see the inside and not just the outside; it is to be mindful of the truth and not just the appearance, and to recognize the whole plane and not just the individual dots. To have prajna-wisdom is to appreciate the Law of Dependent Origination. Venerable Master Huineng, the Sixth Patriarch of the Chan School of Chinese Buddhism, taught that wisdom comes from correcting one's errors and only the unwise will always try to conceal his or her mistakes. Being able to acknowledge one's faults is indeed great wisdom.

A person of wisdom knows to seek the source of life. He or she has the insight to wonder where humans come from and where they go after death. A wise person always sees the main points and disregards matters that are trivial and insignificant. He or she will not waste energy or time haggling over affairs that are private and personal. Thus, people will always respect him or her.

A person of wisdom will not be fazed by crisis. The more pressing the situation, the calmer a person of wisdom remains, because self-composure is the essential ingredient to finding a solution for the problem. A person of wisdom will never be angry, because anger disturbs the inner clarity of wisdom like a rock thrown into a calm lake. If our mind is clouded by negative emotions, we will lose the ability to make proper judgments and cause unnecessary troubles for ourselves.

Truly wise people also understand the importance of reasonable self-effacement. Wise people will exercise self-restraint and not boast about their abilities or lose their patience. They may appear slow-witted, even though they are people of great wisdom.

Although wisdom is a combination of natural endowment and acquired learning, the latter carries much more weight than the former. Through hard work and effort, one can make up any deficiency. Therefore, it is not necessary to be envious of another's cleverness or talents. If we want to reap the fruit, we must first sow the seed. Without sowing the proper causes, our envy of the fruits enjoyed by others will be just that. The most important thing is to have determination and perseverance in our every pursuit, for it is the only way for us to succeed in life. The Buddha says, "Wisdom is prajna and prajna is the path of liberation for ourselves and others."

Stop, Look, and Listen

At railroad crossings, there are signs posted which remind people to "Stop, Look, and Listen." These signs are meant to keep people safe and remind them not to rush across the tracks. Life itself is like a railroad crossing; we should stop, look, and listen at every moment.

During our school years, from elementary school to high school to college, we enjoy vacations in winter and summer, as well as weekends and other holidays. We are always given time to pause, to wait, and to think: which school should I go to next, which courses should I take? Professionally, if we are granted a transfer, a promotion, or even the opportunity to change jobs, we are also given the time to pack and get ready–we can stop, wait, look, and listen. This is important because any step we take in the journey of life is like crossing railroad tracks: danger awaits us if we are careless or take a misstep. Therefore, we should stop and wait for the right moment, listen for any unusual sounds, and also look to see if the red light has turned green to ensure that it is safe to cross.

In dealing with others, we need to stop and think; during the course of our careers, we need to stop and look around us; and regarding our health, we need to remind ourselves to be aware of any possible problems.

To stop is to wait: we wait for our children to grow up, we wait for our careers to develop, and we wait for the right causes and conditions. For any endeavor we intend to undertake, we should wait for the right opportunity to pursue it and the right conditions for it to succeed. We should never stumble rashly into anything. Because when we pause and wait, we are not actually refusing to advance, but instead we are merely proceeding when it is safe to do so. To listen is to assess whether something is good or bad, wholesome or unwholesome. If we don't listen, how can we tell if what is said is good or otherwise. To look is to focus on the target, but when the goal is unclear and its outline fuzzy, it can be like seeing the world without eyes.

In our daily lives, we need to take a break for lunch and get enough

sleep at night, just as machines need to be turned off occasionally for maintenance. In addition to stopping, we also need to listen: we listen for the sound of the bell to get up in the morning at the temple; we listen for reports and for decisions. Sounds come from all around us, so we need to listen carefully in order to understand what is happening.

Stop, so that we can be prepared to have the strength to start over again. Listen, so that we know the responses and sentiments of those around us. Look, so that we are sure of where to go. The railroad crossing may suddenly become impassable due to the presence of a huge locomotive. Since "the capable can always assess the circumstances," it would be foolish to try to resist a powerful force that is impossible to overcome. We should instead take a step back to stop, look, and listen, so as to wait for a better moment to cross. The crossing of life may also be crisscrossed by different kinds of invincible forces; isn't it wise to stop, look, and listen each time you cross?

Gas Station of Life

When you are on the road, you need to stop and refill the car with gas after going certain distances; otherwise, you will not be able to drive on. On the path of life, we also need to refill every so often in order to reach our goals.

Where are the gas stations in life? If we learn from wise teachers and knowledgeable people, they will provide us with encouragement, advice, instructions, or even reproach. If we feel our knowledge is insufficient, we can take courses, attend lectures, or even go back to school. Some people go to libraries or immerse themselves in a temple's sutra archives. All of these are life's gas stations.

Whenever a Buddhist temple is completed and its Buddha hall opened for worship, a gas station for life is built. On our path in life, when we are weary, troubled, or wronged, we can visit a temple and bow before the Buddha in the Buddha hall. The blessing of the Buddha will enter our mind like an infusion of fuel. We can then move forward with renewed energy toward a future with boundless possibilities!

There is potential of fire in wood, but we cannot harness it without lighting it. Our mind becomes like a dark room over the years, and unless the Buddha ignites the light of our hearts for us, the resource inside us will not develop. We cannot be without gas stations just as we cannot be without wise teachers, libraries, and sutras.

Had many renowned Chinese scholars in the past and in the modern age not relied on their faith or on temples as their gas stations in life, they might not have accomplished what they did. Similarly, the Sixth Patriarch Huineng of the Tang Dynasty was encouraged by one Buddhist practitioner and given financial support by another. With such spiritual and material refills, the Chan Master was able to surge ahead in the sea of Dharma, and his life was transformed. Venerable Master Taixu of the Republic Period received a US$3,000 subsidy from the late President Chiang. With the financial aid from Mr. Chiang, Venerable Master Taixu was able to propagate the Dharma around the world and became an international master of Buddhism.

The road of life is a long one. Without refilling ourselves constantly, how can we complete the entire journey? Therefore, none of us can be without gas stations in life!

The Highway of Life

There are numerous highways and freeways in developed countries of the world. Many of these highways are broad and beautiful. Most of us have traveled on these highways and enjoyed the speed, safety, and scenic views they provide. But few have probably thought about the many basic features of highways. For instance, the median strip between the two sides of traffic is often planted with greenery to enhance the view. People have also installed guardrails, blockades, lights, and reflectors to divide the lanes. Then there are shoulders, carpool lanes, emergency lanes, overpasses, speed detectors, phones, electronic billboards, toll-booths, merging lanes, and rest areas. Along the way, there are numerous signs that indicate roads, destinations, distance, speed limits, and rules motorists need to observe.

Life is like a highway. When we are driving on it, we need a median strip to separate us from drivers going in the opposite direction for safety purposes. We need to observe the rules indicated on the road signs and be aware of the reflectors dividing the lanes so that we know on which side we belong. We should not encroach upon others' territory. We must also look out for speed traps, which capture our license plates with cameras should we speed.

Furthermore, we should not drive in carpool lanes when we are alone, nor should we drive on the shoulder. If we need to refresh ourselves or fill up our gas tanks, there are rest areas for us to do so. As in life, if we ignore safety regulations and break the rules, the consequences can be dire.

On highways, it is imperative that we keep a distance between others and ourselves. We must drive at the right speed, not too slow, and never too fast. As in life, there are priorities. What comes first and what comes last should be determined by the guidelines. Seasoned motorists know how to stay out of trouble with the authorities. They slow down at curves and when going under overpasses, they know to watch out for highway patrol waiting on the sides.

All in all, knowing the rules well when driving on the highway is as important as understanding how we should navigate the path of life. When traversing the highway of life we should know that ethics, law, righteousness, conscience, and humility are the best routes to take. Humility and tolerance are the views on the highways. Cause and effect are the rules in moving ahead. Keeping a steady hand on the steering wheel is the key to driving, and reaching home safely is our only goal. If we truly cherish our life, we should indeed drive with care on the highway of life!

Speed Limits

Almost everywhere we go, speed limits are posted. We find them posted on freeways, main roads, and even some back alleys. Speed limits are crucial for safe driving.

In maintaining public safety, the traffic authorities station officers at strategic points with radar and cameras to detect speeding vehicles, since car accidents most commonly occur because of speed limit violations. Therefore, setting speed limits is important.

The roads we drive on can be winding or straight, narrow or wide, smooth or bumpy. The areas we pass through may be densely, moderately, or sparsely populated. Therefore, we need different speed limits for different roads. To set the speed limits, safe driving specialists conduct surveys of road conditions and population densities.

Life is like driving. The distance of our journey depends on many factors. If our physical body were a vehicle, then its age, engine capacity, functions, and speed would all affect how long we could last.

Different cars drive at different speeds. Some can speed up to one hundred miles per hour while others can only sputter along at thirty miles per hour. Likewise, on the journey of life, the quality and speed of the vehicle of our body can differ according to how hard we drive ourselves. Some rush after fame and fortune recklessly and as a result are bound to break down in time. Others drive too slowly, admiring the scenery along the way. When others with newer cars and faster cars overtake us in life, we should recognize our own capacity and not contend with them with abandon.

If life is a vehicle, then we ought to drive it regularly in order to realize its full capacity. If a car is left in the garage or by the roadside too long, it will get rusty and lose its power. Conversely, if we drive it all the time without giving it proper care and maintenance, it will become exhausted just as our bodies would and stall in the middle of a journey.

In addition to the speed we drive, we should also consider load capacity. Overloading a car is unsafe, while carrying too little is wasteful. Therefore, safety and energy conservation are both important factors to consider as we load up our cars. In life, the loads we carry for our families and society also reflect our capacity to benefit others.

Speed limits are for us to follow so that we drive as fast or slow as appropriate. Driving over or below speed limits violates traffic regulations. Overloading is a violation, while refusing to carry any passengers is a waste of energy. The establishment of carpool lanes on America's freeways for vehicles carrying two or more persons is thus a way of maintaining the middle path of proper driving.

The proper way of life can be found within the very concept of speed limits!

The Value of Life

One day, the pig complained to the cow, "Humans are really unfair. While I'm alive, they think of me as dirty, lazy, and stupid. But after I die, they will use my hair, skin, flesh, and even all my organs. But you, cow, are always being praised for your perseverance. This is so unfair to me."

The cow then replied, "While I'm alive I pull carts, till the land, and also provide milk for them. Eventually, I will even contribute my entire body and my skin will be worth much more than yours. But in your case, you have to wait until you die for humans to finally benefit from you–that is the difference between us."

Each of us may be born with individual characteristics and different causes and conditions, but the difference between the value of one person's life and another's depends on the effort of each individual. Therefore, as we grow, we should all shape and plan for our own lives. The meaning of life lies in the contributions and benefits we bring to the world. For instance, the sun shines universally on earth, so everyone likes the sun. Flowing water moistens all living things, so everyone also likes water.

Once, Beethoven was ordered by a prince to perform at a particular place. He walked for three miles in the pouring rain to reach that place, and after his performance, he sent the prince a letter. He wrote, "Your Highness, you became a prince through your good fortune, but I am me because of my own efforts. There might be thousands of princes in the world, but there is only one Beethoven."

Though we are born alike as humans, the value of life is different for each of us because we come from different backgrounds. Sometimes, the value of life is influenced by family, money, and good fortune. But sometimes, the value of life is the result of one's own perseverance and toil. Some are able to benefit society not only while they are alive, but far beyond their lifetimes. For example, Beethoven could play beautiful music when he was alive, but even long after his death he is still being applauded by many.

The value of life lies not in the natural endowments of an individual, but rather, in whether one's life benefits others. A precious diamond may be worth millions, but once somebody owns it and locks it away, then others cannot see its value or worth. On the other hand, worthless rocks used for building roads and bridges provide convenience for everyone passing over them. Therefore, should the value of life be equated to that of a diamond or that of an ordinary rock?

A large mansion may only be occupied by a few members of a family, and outsiders are not able to gain easy access. But a roadside rest stop or a public restroom provides convenience to thousands. Therefore, how can we say that the value of such public places of convenience cannot be compared to that of large beautiful mansions? The value of life depends on how we exercise and express our potential. We should always strive to do so while we are alive. It is all right to be like a pig–only valuable after death; a worse scenario is if we are like dead wood and grass, only good for compost after life is gone. Then the value of our life is too limited. How we realize the value of life is a mission that we all need to work on.

Precious Life

Nature has the virtue of cherishing all life, so that even though there may still be distinctions of wealth and status in this world, ultimately every life is equally precious. Even a small weed growing from a crack in the ground displays the power of life. A fish, when the river runs dry, will seek refuge in the wet mud to preserve its life. By looking at the plants and the animals, we cannot help but get the feeling that like us everything in nature values life. Even the spirit of preserving monuments from the past reflects our instinct of cherishing the life of the past.

Some of us can wear a hat or a coat for eight or ten years, because we know how to cherish the life of things; on the other hand, some people allow their children to trample on new furniture, which could last twenty or thirty years with better care, but instead end up damaged in less than a year. Isn't this not curtailing the life of something useful.

The truth is that everything under the sun has a life of its own. To love is to perpetuate life and liveliness; to love is to support existence and continuation. In Buddhism, this notion of having respect for life in general has been advanced to its fullest extent by advocating equality amongst all beings–"All sentient and non-sentient beings possess the same nature." Thus, it is imperative that we treasure and cherish every situation, every birth and every life.

Nature itself is our life, just as heaven and earth are our parents. The sun and the moon, the mountains and the rivers, creatures that fly and animals that crawl–all of them are our kin, our brothers and sisters. Only by understanding the notion of "being kin to all things" can we truly appreciate the preciousness of life.

A seed can bear infinite fruit; a stream can nourish countless lives. Spring, summer, fall, and winter all play a part in the nurturing of life. Likewise, loving-kindness, compassion, joy, and equanimity are vital to the development of life. The meaning of life is not to pursue a living aimlessly; the purpose of life is not to just seek food and shelter. There is nothing with greater dignity than living; there is nothing more precious than one's life.

To have life is not to waste life; to live is not to live without purpose. The goal is to live life to its fullest extent. The meaning of life does not reside in how long we live nor in the hope of immortality, but in how we choose to make use of every opportunity to enrich the content of our finite life. Although life is ephemeral like a spark rising from burning wood, it can still leave a brilliant, lustrous trail behind.

The ability of material possessions to fulfill us is limited. The nature of human sentiments is inevitably strained and thus cannot assure lasting harmony. Since the physical body is impermanent, time will always bring about the disintegration of the four elements. However, the value of life lies in our ability to welcome a better future by adapting to different causes and conditions.

Even though life being precious is worth cherishing, we must understand that it becomes even more precious when it is sacrificed for a noble and worthy cause. A virtuous person will not seek to live at the expense of his or her humanity. He or she will even give up life to preserve it. A person who is willing to forfeit his or her humanity to preserve life is as good as dead, but one who dies to preserve his or her humanity will leave a legacy that lives on. If we can truly appreciate the value of life and genuinely understand its preciousness, then we will have no trouble seeing how wonderful the world can be.

The Code of Life

Scientists have already deciphered the code of life by unlocking the secret of human DNA. From a Buddhist perspective, the code of life or DNA has another name–karma. The Buddha taught the world about it more than 2,500 years ago. If we consider the code of life merely as DNA, then it is no more than an unit or a cell, and is not enough to explain life. The truth of karma would provide a more comprehensive explanation.

Karma is the action of the body, speech, and mind. There is wholesome, unwholesome, and neutral karma. "Even going through thousands of kalpas, the karma created never dies." All the karma generated by the body, speech, and mind will be stored in the warehouse of karma, the way a computer stores information. "When the causes and conditions ripen, karmic retribution will be experienced by the self." The Law of Karma is immutable. What goes around comes around–it may ripen tomorrow, next month, or many years from now, but it is inevitable.

Karmic power is one of the Buddha's great realizations. Humans live from previous lives to the current one, and then carry on to future lives. The crucial link in all this is karmic power, which strings the ongoing lives together like a rope. Nothing is missing; nothing is lost. Because of karma, life never ends. "Water from the spring rains flows along toward the east." Similarly, the seasons change with time, spring comes and fall goes, and along with them, the warm weather and the cool breezes. Everything comes and goes in cycles and is reborn. Any conditioned dharmas can be destroyed, but only the code of life is indestructible and exists infinitely.

DNA can only explain the components of an individual life. But, according to Buddhism, there is not only individual karma; there is also collective karma. For instance, the reason for so many individuals being born in the same family, the same village, or the same tribe is "collective karma." But when people from different walks of life experience an accident while traveling on a ship or a plane, some dying while others survive are examples of "individual karma" within "collective karma." So even though scientists have already discovered DNA as the code of life for the individual, we hope they will further determine the common factors among living beings, a theory that can explain the unity of all life.

Because of variations in DNA, different lives are formed. Our karmic power, however, manifests in different ways. There is karma that is generated and arrives in this life, like planting in the spring and harvesting in the fall. Then, there is karma that is generated in this life but arrives in the next life, like planting this year and harvesting next year. Last but not least, there is also the karma that is generated in this life but doesn't arrive until some life beyond the next life, like a harvest that is planted this year and harvested a number of years later. So, karma always manifests itself; it is just a matter of time.

The truths of causes and conditions, karma, and karmic retribution in Buddhism are indisputable truths, absolute, universal, and equal for all. The discovery of DNA by scientists merely serves to explain the content and function of karma more concretely.

The Three Dimensions of Life

In life, there are three very important dimensions. If we handle them well, we will live a happy and peaceful life. Otherwise, we will have endless troubles. The three dimensions are time, space, and human relations.

The first dimension is time. Being punctual is very important. We must always be on time for any appointment. Time is of the essence in life. We often see "guaranteed next-day delivery," "one-hour photo," or "same-day service." We may have heard the saying, "Every day I tear off a page from my desk calendar, my heart grows more and more anxious." This is because the time available in life is so limited. Days whiz by and the years follow right after. How long does life last? How can we not take time seriously?

The second dimension is space. Space is very important in life. From a very young age, we learned to fight for a place to sit or even a bed to sleep in. We always want a little more space for ourselves. In society, we contend for land or for a house all for the sake of gaining more space. How many people nowadays end up going to court over matters of space? When people argue after a car accident, they are actually fighting over space; who had right of way or was first entitled to the space in which the collision occurred? Many countries go to battle over airspace or land. As a result, many people are killed and injured. Even though the universe is vast and wide and we take up no more than an area of eight feet when we sleep at night, who is willing to give up some space?

The third dimension is human relations. If we get along well with others by helping one another, we enjoy much happiness. However, if we envy or reject each other, then we suffer. It is important that we should have respect, tolerance, understanding, and support for one another. If one side fails to understand and forgive what another side has done, then problems will ensue. When a loving couple ends up in divorce, it shows their relationship was not well-managed. If age-old friends become enemies, their relationship must have had problems. Therefore, if the relationship between self and others is inappropriate or unreasonable, there will be trouble.

In reality, every person is only half of any relationship or even just a third of it. Other than the self, there is also you. Other than you, there is still him or her. And then there are also the many different kinds of people around us that we come in contact with. Human relations are indeed difficult to handle!

In reviewing the three dimensions of life, we see that although we can manage our own time, we cannot control time itself. As for space, we each have our own place. Since every inch of space has an owner, we cannot unlawfully claim any. In human relations, we need to depend on our wisdom, skills, merits, and conditions. We must learn to contribute sufficiently to the world in order to have peace and harmony. If we can harmonize human relations, we gain peace and happiness. Therefore, how we deal with the three dimensions in life depends on our wisdom and cultivation.

A Complete and Balanced Life

There are two kinds of lives: a life that is finite and measurable and a life that is infinite that is non-arising and non-ceasing. Buddhas have two kinds of bodies: Transformation-body–(nirmanakaya) and Dharma-body (dharmakaya). The Transformation-body is the body of a Buddha, characterized by thirty-two marks of excellence and eighty accessory marks, and it is also subject to birth and death. The Dharma-body is the body of Dharma. It embodies the teachings of a Buddha and exists everywhere, at all times. The Dharma-body vertically penetrates past, present, and future; horizontally it covers the ten directions, and is characterized by the four transcendental realities of nirvana–permanence, happiness, self, and purity–that are not subject to arising and ceasing.

Although, as sentient beings, we have not yet realized the Dharma-body, we can apply its meaning to our lives. For example, we can broaden our horizons in all directions to have a life that is expansive. We can also engage in various exchanges and interactions to have a life that penetrates the past, present, and future. In this world of ten directions, there are an unlimited number of fascinating and beautiful things to discover. For example, we can familiarize ourselves with astronomy, geography, science, and philosophy. We should take interest in the world's wonderful things and interesting people, not leaving any stone unturned or any grass unexamined.

To have a life that penetrates the three time periods, we must be spiritually connected with the sages and events of the past, in addition to staying in touch with the world's people. Today, with the help of the internet and electronic mail, we have finally built a communication network that allows us to easily communicate with people around the world without leaving the comfort of home. Is this not living a life that "penetrates the three time periods and pervades the ten directions"?

In fact, we can apply this principle to how we should deal with others and handle matters. For example, when we come across a piece of information that is important for everyone to have, we must make sure that it is communicated to everybody involved. When we take up a task, we must maintain effective communication or we will face opposition and pressure from those around us. Therefore, in dealing with human affairs, we must have both broad interactions and inclusive relationships. If we want our lives to run smoothly with our peers, superiors, and subordinates, we must establish harmonious relationships with people and show that we care at all times. We cannot allow the distance of space or the passage of time to become excusable obstacles.

At first glance, the city of Los Angeles, with its crisscrossing freeways, looks like a giant spider web. However, when we take a closer look, we find that the roads are numbered in such a way as to indicate directions. All northbound and southbound freeways are assigned odd numbers, and all eastbound and westbound highways are given even numbers. Our lives should be like the freeway system of a big city; although it is complicated, it can be more complete with rules and regulations.

When we weave a piece of cloth, the threads are woven into it horizontally and vertically. When we put up a building, steel beams run crossways and perpendicular. When our body is too wide, we will not be happy if we continue to expand horizontally; if it is too thin, we will also not want it to keep stretching upward. The best is for everything to develop horizontally and vertically in a balanced manner.

Our universe is made up of vertical time and horizontal space. If we are to have a complete and balanced life, we need to make good use of time and space, paying close attention and learning to be flexible.

Life's Dictionary

Have you checked out the dictionary of life? Do you know what it is? It is the book of our lives from birth into this world until we bid farewell. From past to present, there has not been a life dictionary just for some people. In fact, everyone has his or her own life dictionary. Life's dictionary does not only record this life of ours, it also records all the good and bad that we have done, said, and thought from past lives to the endless future. We can find all of these in life's dictionary.

Napoleon once said that the word "difficulty" was not in his lexicon; and Socrates did not have "suffering" in his. Consequently, both became models through the ages. Self-serving politicians only have power in their dictionaries, loyal ministers their countries, lovers love, parents their children, and Buddhas and bodhisattvas all sentient beings. Of all these dictionaries, some are rich and varied, and interesting to examine. However, some lack substance, attracting no one to turn the pages.

There are many kinds of dictionaries, just as there are different professions in the world: medicine, science, philosophy, astronomy, geography, etc. Among people, there is also a broad range of types. There are loyal ministers, renowned generals, cowards, devoted children, the wise, and the mean.

In our lives, as the cells of our physical bodies multiply and divide, and our wisdom and spirits develop, they are also full of vocabulary. For instance, in some people's lives, compassion takes up half of their dictionaries. For others, their dictionaries are filled with the fragrance of wisdom.

A dictionary is a silent teacher, a recap of our lives, and a display of our efforts. A good dictionary would reflect our responsibility to country, family, and oneself. So, we must compile it with the strength of our vows, compassion, wisdom, ideals, and aspirations.

Our dictionaries should be made up of many words of inspiration that can contribute to the community. They should be filled with dedication, contribution, benevolence, honor, respect, integrity, practicality, frugality, tolerance, joy, harmony, ethics, and diligence, so that they can be passed on for generations and the pages happily turned and discovered by many over time.

Cause and Effect in the Three Time Periods

Facing life's mysteries, some ask, "What did I do in my past life?" Others wonder, "What will happen in my future life?" There are those who bitterly protest the injustices of life because people fail to realize the truth of cause and effect. The Buddha said, "If we want to know the cause of the past, all we need to do is to look at the effect of the present. If we want to know the effect of the future, all we need to do is to look at what we have done in the present." In other words, the past is the cause of the present, and the present the cause of the future. Causes of the past bring about effects of the present, and causes of the present will determine the effects of the future. This is the basic meaning of the Law of Cause and Effect in the three time periods.

"One will reap what one has sown" is a simple truth. The concept of "what goes around comes around" is very clear. But there are still those who fail to understand the Law of Cause and Effect. The reason behind this lack of understanding can be attributed to the examples of those who have enjoyed a life of luxury despite their evil deeds, while others suffer a life of misery despite their virtuous character. If people do not seem to get what they deserve, then why should anyone have faith in karmic retribution?

In truth, the implications of the Law of Cause and Effect pervades the three time periods and so cannot be understood by looking at just one period. Its logic is very simple: if a person previously made numerous deposits in a bank, we have no right to refuse a withdrawal based on his or her present bad deeds. Likewise, if a person borrowed a lot of money in the past, we cannot cancel all his or her debts in light of his present moral cultivation. When it comes to the effects of karma, there are those that are experienced in this lifetime, but some are also experienced in the next life or in many subsequent future lives. Every good deed will be rewarded, and every bad deed punished; the only question is when and where.

Moreover, "cause and effect" has its own principle. For example, our health is based on the Law of Cause and Effect. If one wants to be healthy, he or she cannot just pray to the Buddha and do good deeds. He or she must eat well, live healthily, and keep his or her mind happy and worry free. He or she must have the right habits to be healthy. Likewise, if we want to be wealthy, we must work hard. If we want to have a good reputation, we must cultivate good virtue and have good character. We must not confuse one cause with another. We must remember that for each effect, there is a corresponding cause or set of causes. To be healthy, we must have healthy causes. To be virtuous, we must have virtuous causes. To be wealthy, we must have wealthy causes. And to be faithful to our beliefs, we must have the cause of faith.

Between cause and effect, there are also conditions. Although cause and effect have an inevitable relationship, the arising of conditions can alter the nature of that relationship. For example, when we plant a fruit tree, the seed will determine what kind of fruit we get, but conditions such as the quality of the soil and weather will also determine the final size and sweetness of the fruit we harvest. Therefore, we must have faith in the Law of Cause and Effect and the principle of karmic retribution.

A person's life is beginningless in the chain of rebirth. It is also endless. We are continuously reborn in the three time periods of past, present, and future. With each rebirth, we carry with us all the karma that we have incurred since beginningless time. All the miseries of the present, every gain and loss, are effects of the past and causes of the future. In this way, the Law of Cause and Effect is inescapable and does not make any exceptions.

The Future Is Better than the Past

Most people love a trip down memory lane. They yearn for the past with a tinge of pleasure, because they believe the past is better than the present. However, time passes and things change. In a blink of an eye, everything will be different. Although the setting sun might be immeasurably sweet, dusk is only nearing. Therefore, we cannot always dwell on the past. If we want a better tomorrow, we should look forward to the future and broaden our horizons without indulging in nostalgia.

Once, there was a puppy that ran in circles all day long chasing its own tail. A big dog walked by and was puzzled by what it saw. It asked the puppy what it was doing. The puppy replied, "Haven't you heard that a dog's happiness is in its tail? By chasing it, I am going after happiness. Don't you want happiness in your life?" The big dog said, "All I know is that if I just walk forward with all my might, happiness will follow me closely." Therefore, we must live in hope and not in our memories, for the future is more beautiful than the past; it holds immeasurable potential!

In life, everyone experiences difficulty as well as satisfaction. When things are going well, we must take them lightly in stride. When faced with adversity, we must forbear whatever comes our way. As long as we can bear down and weather the storm, it will eventually pass. Even if we have failed miserably in the past, we must not be discouraged, because past failures are the best lessons for future success. If we learn from our mistakes and make good connections with others, we will be on our way to a promising future.

According to the Buddhist notion of cause and effect in the three time periods–the past, present, and future–life is not limited to just one term. Because of the past, we have the present. Because of the present, we have the future. Because of the future, we have the three time periods of the past, the present, and the future. Because of the three time periods, we have hope. As long as we live with hope, tomorrow will be a better day.

It is hard to judge whether one's life is a success or a failure at any given time. We may be unsuccessful in how we handle affairs, but we should never fail in how we conduct ourselves. We may fail in our past, but not in our future. No matter how brilliant we once might have been, we cannot assume that the recognition we have received in the past is lasting. What is important is what we accomplish now. Yet, the "present" will become the "past" as soon as it arrives, while the next moment will become the "present." Therefore, we should not be overly pleased with what we have achieved. Our actions must adhere to the principles of beauty, truth, and goodness. Our future will definitely be better if we can continuously improve and adapt ourselves.

If we want to progress in life, we should not limit ourselves. We should keep striving for advancement and breakthroughs without indulging ourselves in past accomplishments. Nobody can help us if we refuse to let go and only live for the past. It does not matter what our achievements might have been in the past. It does not matter how popular we were yesterday. They are occurrences of the past. We should concentrate our efforts on the present for the sake of having a brighter future. Without question, the future is much better than the past. It is full of endless possibilities!

How Many Years of Life?

How many years should we live? How about a hundred and twenty? But, if we live to a hundred and twenty years old, we would probably suffer the loss of our children, and even our grandchildren might be nearing death. When the old have to see the young die, is life any better?

At a hundred and twenty years old, we will not be able to walk, our teeth will be gone, and our eyes will hardly be able to see. Will we be happy then? Therefore, longevity itself should not be the true meaning of life. If living to one hundred and twenty years old is meaningless, then what about half of it, say sixty years old? That is usually a time when we are accomplished professionally and our halls filled with children and grandchildren. Life before that time is a lot of hard work, but sixty is the age to enjoy its fruit. Thus, ending life at that point would seem like such a pity.

How many years we should live is a difficult question to answer. If we do not contribute to society and are not very happy with our lives, even two or three hundred years of life would be meaningless. On the other hand, if we have joy and ease in our lives and serve our communities well, then regardless of how long we live, we will leave fond memories behind. In that case, we need not care too much about how many years we actually live.

Venerable Master Sengzhao and Yan Hui both lived to only thirty-one years old. However, history books and the people who came after praised them for their achievements and the effect they had on later generations. In this sense, their legacy not only lasted very long, but they remained deep in the mind of posterity.

Since ancient times, many beauties have died in the prime of their youth and many gifted scholars perished in their blooming years due to some unforeseeable accident. How long then should we live? We cannot answer this question just by considering the notion of lifespan in terms of years. We should evaluate life by the legacy of one's career, writings, merits, morals, and faith. Longevity should therefore be assessed by the level of contribution to the world and not by time. In looking at histori-

cal figures, Jesus lived to thirty-three, First Emperor of Qin forty-nine, Emperor Taizong of the Tang Dynasty fifty-three, Dr. Sun Yat-Sen sixty, Mohammed sixty-two, the Buddha eighty, and the Honored Ananda, the Buddha's attendant, Chan Master Zhaozhou, and Elder Monk Xuyun all lived to a hundred and twenty.

From these historical figures we can see that the number of years we live is irrelevant. Compared to our physical bodies, values of compassion, morals, speech, and careers are much more important.

The Thirty Years of Human Life

The following parable on the thirty years of human life is quite thought-provoking: The King of Hell was handing out sentences during a hearing. When the prisoner Zhao was brought before him, he exclaimed, "Zhao! You were righteous and generous as a human, and you were virtuous and well-cultivated, so you can now be reborn as a human again for a lifespan of thirty years." Upon hearing this, Zhao gratefully thanked the king and moved to one side.

The king then pounded his gavel and proclaimed to the next in line, "Qin! You were selfish and deluded in your human life. Not knowing the truth, you held deviant views and were lazy and slothful. You are now to be reborn in the human world as a cow for thirty years." Qin was devastated upon hearing his sentence and appealed to the king, "A cow has to do a lot of hard work, pulling carts and tilling the land. Thirty years is way too long for me. I could only carry on for fifteen." The king asked, "What should we do with the remaining fifteen then?" Zhao came forward and knelt in front of the king, requesting, "Please give the cow's fifteen years to me." The king agreed and Zhao's human life was extended to forty-five years.

Then the king cried out the sentence to the next one, "Sun! You were ignorant of cause and effect as a human. Being blindly loyal to your superiors, you took advantage of the kind and gentle. You are now to be reborn in the human world as a dog for thirty years." To this Sun responded, "King, dogs usually eat leftovers and watch the house all day long. Sometimes people even kick them around or hit them with a stick. It is too tough. I think fifteen years is all I could handle!" Zhao again came forward and immediately asked, "King, please give the dog's fifteen years to me as well!" So his human lifespan was increased from forty-five to sixty years.

The king continued on with his sentencing and shouted, "Li! You were cunning and devious as a human, never engaged in any proper business, and simply lived off others. You are now to be reborn in the human world as a monkey for thirty years." Li was scared out of his wits and implored, "King, a monkey lives in the woods and has to endure the elements. There is only fruit for food, and there is also the threat of the hunters' arrows. Such a life of fear is too hard to bear; fifteen years is all I could take!" Zhao again came forward and pled, "King, please allow me to take the monkey's fifteen years!" Therefore, he could now live to seventy-five years.

This parable suggests that we really only have thirty prime years of carefree life. Throughout the remaining years, we have burdens and responsibilities that we did not have before. We will slave like the cow bringing up our children, then we will eat leftovers like the dog and wait up for them when they go out, and finally, we will live out our days like the monkey filled with the fear of death. That is because after thirty years, the rest of life will resemble that of the cow, the dog, and the monkey.

In living our life in this world, we should have wisdom, righteousness, and kindness, and should not commit any unwholesome deeds, for the years of a human life are all based on cause and effect!

The Stairway of Life

In this modern age, with developments in science and medicine, the quality of life is much enhanced. The residents of developed nations enjoy an average lifespan of eighty years. Our eighty-year lifespan can be compared to an eighty-story building. After being born, we live year by year, as though we were climbing the building one floor at a time. In the long journey of life, how are we going to climb to the top of the eighty-story building? How are we going to reach the pinnacle of life?

Once, there were two brothers who went mountain climbing. Upon returning home, which was located on the eightieth floor of a high-rise building, they found that the elevator had broken down. With their mountain-climbing experience, they felt they could easily manage eighty floors. Though they were tired, they resolved to make their way up the stairway. When they reached the twentieth floor, they discovered they were not tired at all, and felt they were so good at mountain climbing that even a tall building was nothing to worry about. But as they continued their ascent up to the fortieth floor, they started to feel tired, especially with all the heavy mountain-climbing gear they were carrying. So, they decided to leave their baggage on the fortieth floor and come back for it after the elevator became available again.

On the strength of their confidence and courage, they continued their climb. By the time they reached the sixtieth floor, they finally felt fatigued. Short of breath and worn out, they could not continue. But when they stopped to think, "Home is only twenty more floors away," complcting the climb didn't seem so difficult. So, despite their condition–the sweat, breathlessness, and sore muscles–they still overcame the difficulties and made it to the eightieth floor. As they were about to open their front door, the older brother suddenly exclaimed, "Oh no! The keys are in our baggage!" At this point, both brothers were completely deflated!

The moral of the story is: of the eighty stories of life, the first twenty stories are a breeze. We are young and happy, and our futures look bright. By forty, the burden of family and raising children becomes so heavy for some that they leave it behind to continue on to sixty. At that time, with failing physical strength, the burden of life will become even harder to bear. But, as life should move onwards and upwards, we carry on with the aging body. By the time eighty is reached, we may reflect on the past and the key that we left on the fortieth floor. But by then, our strength would have waned so much that we can no longer go back for it to open up the door to our happy home.

Wise readers, you also have an eighty-story life. What would you like to do at each floor?

Limitless Life

Once, a rich man was celebrating his sixtieth birthday and invited a Chan master to pray for longevity on his behalf. The Chan master asked him, "How many more years of life would you like to ask for?"

The rich man paused and replied, "Maybe twenty more years!"

The Chan master said, "You are already sixty, twenty more years will make you only eighty. Wouldn't that be too few!"

"So you mean I can get more? Let me live to a hundred then!" the man exclaimed.

The Chan master again explained, "A hundred is only forty more years. That would go by very quickly!"

"Do you mean I can ask for a hundred and twenty?"

"A hundred and twenty is still only sixty more years. You are already sixty, adding another sixty years is not much!"

The rich man asked, "So what should we do?"

The Chan master replied, "You should ask for limitless life!"

Life does not end! The human body is born and is extinguished, but life itself does not!

We all have a life that does not end, which is our original intrinsic nature! We often hear people say, "May you live to be a hundred!" Or even "May you live to a hundred and twenty!" But is living to a hundred and twenty really a good thing? By the time we are a hundred and twenty, our hundred-year-old son may already be dead, and our eighty-year-old grandson may also have passed away. How would we feel seeing our younger kin pass away before our eyes? At a hundred and twenty, we would have difficulties eating and walking. We would not see or hear well. What fun is there in life then?

There is a saying, "It is rare to live to seventy." Others say, "Life begins at seventy." Actually, life does not end even at seventy, and it does not begin there either. Life actually has no beginning or end.

Once, a young man asked an elder whose hair was all silvery white how old he was. The old man replied, "Four!" The young man thought he was being funny and joking with him. The senior explained, "I speak the truth! I lived aimlessly for many years; it is only in the last four years that I realized the meaning of life lies in serving and benefitting others. The last four years of life have been truly meaningful for me. So, this is why I say I am only four."

After this lifespan, we still have the next one, or even limitless ones. Just like a flower that has withered, as long as its seeds remain, it will live a second, third, and potentially endless number of lives. The human physical body is conditioned dharma, so it is subject to the cycle of birth and death. But life itself and our spirit are non-conditioned dharmas, which have limitless lives.

"Limitless Life" is the name of Amitabha Buddha. Amitabha Buddha is not only "Limitless Life" but also "Limitless Light." Limitless life transcends time, and limitless light transcends space. If we can pour our spirit, wisdom, and contribution into limitless time and space, won't we then be able to also enjoy limitless lives?

The Planting of Perspective

In a person's life, there are many key factors that can determine one's success and failure. Having a correct or flawed point of view is one of the most important factors. Some people are so steeped in the idea of making money that nothing else matters. They will even set aside good character and morality in the pursuit of money, but in the end they will achieve nothing of significance.

Having a "point of view" is like planting a seed in that what we reap will depend on what point of view we sow. A wholesome perspective will lead to wealth, success, and even great virtue, whereas an unwholesome one will only lead to decrepitude and moral decay. Having a sound perspective is like having wealth that can be enjoyed forever. There are many sayings:

"A person's value comes from one's contributions; a person's legacy comes from pursuing greatness."

"To use money is to have money; to have money is a kind of merit. Knowing how to use money properly is wisdom."

"A person must have an image of the virtuous for the sake of emulating him."

"To be the first, one must learn to be the second; to be the boss, one must learn to be the subordinate."

"To have a good crop, one must first plow the earth and sow the seeds; to be treated well by others, one must first treat others with trust and respect."

One's growth depends on the soundness of one's perspective. One will only make progress if one can learn to adjust one's perspective. The quality of our perspective is also the basis of our relationships with others. Whether or not we can exert a positive influence on others comes down to how acceptable our perspective is to the majority of people.

The right perspective is wealth just as the Buddha's teachings are the most precious Dharma treasure. However, many in the past have misconstrued Buddhism. If we are willing to study, to understand, to have the correct perception of, and to practice the Dharma, we will have the treasure of the Dharma forever. We will reap infinite benefits. In the six perfections or paramitas, "giving charity" is perceived as giving to others, but in reality, it is a way to gain inner wealth. "Upholding the precepts" is perceived as restriction, but it is a way to true freedom and safety. "Patience" is perceived as suffering a loss, but it is a way to gain advantage. "Diligence" is perceived as something hard, but it is a way to happiness and success. "Meditation" is perceived as something boring, but it is a way to vivacity and tranquility. "Wisdom" is often confused with cleverness, but it is the insightful realization of the truth.

In the five precepts, "no killing" is the rule against taking another's life. "No stealing" prohibits taking another's possessions. "No sexual misconduct" forbids the violation of another's body. "No lying" is the rule against damaging another's good name, and "no intoxication" prohibits the infringement on one and others. If the five precepts can be observed faithfully, the true manifestation of freedom and democracy will result.

In this world, everything happens in a moment of thought. If our minds develop an inclination towards the true, the good, and the beautiful, our lives will be enriched beyond imagination. If we are willing to examine our perspective and introspect daily, our characters will be vastly improved. By broadening our horizons and revising our point of view constantly, we will become better people.

Morality is the key to maintaining successful relationships. The integrity of our characters depends on our virtue. The more virtuous we are, the more respectable we will be. Positive thinking is the foundation of loving-kindness and generosity. If we can produce within ourselves correct understanding, pure thoughts, and admirable aspirations, and if we can speak words that will bring joy to others like sunshine and flowers, we will definitely have a wonderful life.

To Adjust One's Views

Views are, of course, the way we look at things–so if we look at things positively then everything is well. If we like something, then we will consider it good no matter what. After all, beauty is in the eye of the beholder. Conversely, if we have no faith in what we see, then even if we come face to face with a sage, we will perceive him as merely another stubborn old person. Therefore, subjective views exert tremendous influence on the individual.

Someone once asked, "Where is heaven and where is hell?" They are of course all in one's views! If we are content with what we have, even a simple dwelling is as good as heaven. But when there is no contentment, then even the most luxurious mansion will be like hell. Therefore, whether we experience heaven or hell entirely hinges upon our viewpoint.

An investor went to Africa to start a business and upon seeing everyone going around barefoot; he thought a shoe factory would be a good investment. When his partner went to look at the site, he commented, "Africans all go around barefoot; they're not used to wearing shoes. If we come here to make shoes, where will our business come from?" He then left for home. Therefore, a single view can make or break something, bring progress or cause retreat.

When we view things with the light of hope, then everything glows. When we view things with the confidence of success, then we will enjoy success in anything we do. When our views are constructive, then we will not sabotage good efforts or good people. When we view everything with goodness, then everything will be so. Therefore, human views are a garden in which fragrant, beautiful flowers can abound, or a factory that can produce beneficial goods to help others. When there is hope in our views, then we are able to build many projects of hope.

Views can have the capacity to encompass the universe and create limitless dharma realms. However, there are some who hold pessimistic and passive views, or they wish to get everything for nothing. Or, some may be totally unrealistic, always looking for instant results. How is it possible for them to live life well? So, whether we want to live life with smiles on our faces or shed tears constantly entirely depends on how we view life.

We need not look for fame and fortune. Instead, we only need to build up good, truthful, benevolent, and beautiful views. Because when we have positive views as the cause, then we will not need to worry about whether or not we will reap good fruit.

A Sense of Mission in Life

People often ask, "Why do we live in this world? What is the meaning of life?" The answer to these questions is, "Humans have a mission in this world, and the meaning of life lies in their sense of mission!"

Different people have different missions in life. Some people vow to serve their country. Others want to benefit their family by establishing a business. There are people who appreciate the importance of education and dedicate themselves to teaching. Then there are others who think of serving the community by manufacturing products.

Parents take educating their children as their mission and are willing to work hard toward that end. Some spouses make sacrifices in order to help their partners succeed. Soldiers in battle are prepared to die for their country. Teachers spend their lives teaching and lecturing in class. Medical professionals work around the clock to save lives and alleviate suffering. Religious leaders live a life of simplicity so as to spread the truth and liberate all sentient beings. In addition, truckers and drivers transport people and goods day and night; journalists and reporters risk their lives in order to get to the truth; and actors laugh and cry in performances to entertain their audiences. They all have missions in life.

People need a mission in life. There are, however, many who do not have any sense of mission. They spend their days doing nothing but eating and playing. They loiter here and there, never take a proper job, sometimes even make a living by swindling and cheating. Without a sense of purpose, their lives have little meaning.

Even animals have a mission. Dogs watch homes and guide the blind. Cats catch mice, roosters crow at dawn, bees pollinate plants, oxen pull carts, and horses carry riders for miles. As human beings, how can we possibly have no mission in life?

People Need Ideals

According to *Humble Table, Wise Fare*, "First-rate people act with sublime ideals. Second-rate people act with common sense according to their experiences. Third-rate people act according to their needs and desires. Fourth-rate people act to hurt others." Most of today's youth lack ideals and ambition. Because they do not make vows, and lack passion, mindfulness, and aspirations, they do not show much drive.

When we have ideals, we will not find work difficult, nor will we be calculating when holding the short end of the stick. With ideals, we can overcome difficulties and find great strength in life. Therefore, we need ideals in order to have ambition, aspirations, passion, and accomplishments.

Ideals are noble hopes; and we should have many hopes in life. Hope leads us onto the right path and directs us toward our goals. The worst tragedy in life is hopelessness. A life without hope offers us a dim, gray future.

Even dogs and cats hope for three meals a day, and plants and flowers look for the daily moistening of morning dew. As humans, the highest order of living beings, how can we not have noble hopes and sublime ideals? When we have ideals in life, we have the strength to progress. A life without ideals is like a dry brook where nothing will grow. A life without ideals is like a desert where no living things can survive. With ideals, we have the opportunity to grow, and life can carry on.

Mountain climbers are able to conquer the highest mountains because of their ideals. Seafarers can traverse the vast oceans because of their hope. Humans can land on the moon because of their commitment to explore space. A Chan practitioner can concentrate during meditation because of the wish to discover the secret world of the mind. So many great ventures in the world are accomplished on the strength of ideals and wishes.

There are also some people who want to attain Buddhahood. They hope to become sages, hermits, or heroes. All in all, people need ideals so that life can be bright. People need ideals so there is motivation. With ideals, life becomes meaningful and filled with optimism. With ideals, we can live in a world of endless possibilities.

Cultivating the Field of the Mind

In ancient China, owning arable land was the safeguard against famine. Land has always been a lifeline of the Chinese. It has been the most important inheritance that is passed on from one generation to the next. Unfortunately, some children do not appreciate the intentions of their forefathers. They often fail to cultivate the land well, or allow the fields to lie fallow for good. Worse yet, they sell off pieces of the land here and there at low prices. This behavior is truly regrettable. We need to fully utilize and cultivate these fields.

More importantly, we need to cultivate and develop the field of our mind. How do we cultivate our mind? Buddhism teaches us to develop and sow seeds in the field of our mind by making vows.

In the world today, we often see new land reclaimed from the sea or from polluted, abandoned industrial areas. We can plant trees and crops, construct buildings, or even store materials on this reclaimed land, but how do we cultivate our mind? What can we plant there? There are a number of things we can do. We can use thoughts, contemplation, reflection, calmness, and recitation of the Buddhas' names, to name a few. We can also use meditative concentration, study, repentance, and vows. It is easy to till the land but difficult to cultivate the mind field; it can only be achieved with our vows.

One day, when the Buddha went out to beg for alms, he met a Brahman working in a field. Upon seeing the Buddha, the Brahman questioned, "Buddha, why don't you till your own land and make a living with your labor?"

The Buddha smiled and replied, "I cultivate diligently every moment!"

The Brahman was puzzled, "Well, I never see you using a plough, yoke, or shovel to till the land."

With compassion, the Buddha explained, "All sentient beings are my land, faith my seeds, the Dharma my water, wisdom my sunshine, upholding the precepts my plough, diligent practice my ox, right mindfulness the rope guiding my ox, the truth my handle, the three karmas are the weeds to be removed, and the pure joy of nirvana the fruit of my cultivation."

As the saying goes, "Weeds of ignorance should never grow in the field of the mind. Flowers of wisdom should always blossom in the land of nature." What we reap depends on what we sow. Whether we want to grow compassion and wisdom or ignorance and deviant views all depends on what we plant in our mind. If we want to reap the fruit of intelligence, skillfulness, insight, and understanding, then we should plant seeds of wisdom. If we want to harvest the crop of connection, harmony, peace, and ease, then we need to sow seeds of compassion.

We must plough the field of our mind before we seed, grow, and harvest. We should use the vows of improvement to plough the mind, the resolve to let go of attachments to cultivate it, and the bodhi mind to seed it. Since we all have the treasures of compassion, wisdom, faith, strength, and humility in our mind, in our cultivation, we need to be compassionate toward others and diligent in our practice in order to improve our beings and lessen our worries. Only those who are willing to cultivate their mind are able to discover their intrinsic nature and progress on the path to Buddhahood.

Coping with Problems

What are our problems in life? From an individual standpoint, we have problems with school, friends, marriage, work, finances, health, as well as aging, sickness, and death. From a family standpoint, we face problems supporting our family members, caring for and loving our parents, relating to relatives and neighbors, and receiving community support. From a social standpoint, there are problems concerning public roles, duty, rights, social participation, and loyalty to the country.

Problems are inevitable, and once they arise, we should face them and look for solutions. The following are some approaches to finding solutions:

1. Be honest and keep promises. We should be honest and keep our word. When confronted with problems, we should speak out and explain our positions. We cannot solve any problem by being deceitful, because we will only end up jeopardizing the situation further.

2. Be kind and friendly. Whether or not a problem can be solved depends on human relations. It is only through kindness and friendliness that problems can be solved smoothly. On the contrary, our hostile facial expressions, attitudes, or even pretentiousness only serve to complicate matters, making them more difficult to resolve.

3. Be considerate of others. Being considerate of another's position is an essential element in resolving problems. It requires mutual effort to reach solutions, but if we do not take the initiative to help others with their difficulties, then how can we expect them to work with us? Therefore, when both sides insist on their own positions, problems can never be fully addressed. Besides, without two-way communication, we only complicate matters and prevent ourselves from finding a solution.

4. Learn to accept disadvantages. Those who learn to embrace disadvantages are actually the greatest and wisest. As the saying goes, "We must endure in order to succeed and to accomplish." So, if we are willing to accept disadvantages, we will surely resolve our problems.

Once we are equipped with these approaches, we will be in an advantageous position. With honesty and trust, we will have no problem finding jobs. When we are kind and friendly, we will enjoy friendship everywhere. If we take the initiative to help others when they are in financial troubles, feeling inadequate, struggling with a physical disability, or lacking positive causes and conditions, they will certainly be happy to accept our kindness. Between siblings and parents in a family, and among friends and colleagues, we should learn to accept disadvantages. People are more likely to help us if we learn to do so.

Therefore, when we are confronted with problems, if we simply show our sincerity in finding solutions, any situation can be resolved.

Do Not Wait

Things that can be completed in this life should not be left for the next one. Matters that can be taken care of today should not be put off until tomorrow. Tasks that we can do ourselves should not be left to others. Sometimes, we need to wait for the right opportunities and conditions to ripen, and our strength needs time to be nurtured; however, taking the initiative and realizing vows cannot wait!

When the occasion requires specific conditions and the cooperation of others, we need to wait. If the rice is not yet cooked, we should not lift the lid of the pot. If baby chicks are not yet ready to hatch, the mother hen will not peck at the shells.

The fool invited guests over and waited for them to arrive before he milked his cows, but by then, there was no more milk. On the contrary, Chan Master Daoyuan dried mushrooms in the noon sun; of course, he did it when the sun was high and not after it had set.

More importantly, in helping others or doing good deeds, we should never procrastinate! When we have the ability or money to perform charity, we should not hesitate to do so. Often, it is only when we lose all our possessions in a fire or natural disaster that we realize wealth is always subject to the five common threats of despotic rulers, thieves, floods, fire, and profligate children.

Anything that we can do ourselves, we should not wait for others to do; others are not the same as us. We can build a house on a piece of land that we own, but if we wait for our children to grow up hoping that they will build the house, we may be disappointed because they may sell the land. Anything that can be done today, we should do, because there is no guarantee that tomorrow will arrive. We should do charity work when we are able to do so and never wait until we become wealthy because life is impermanent. When the blossoms are in bloom we should go see them right away before they wither. Do not "wait until we have time" because we may never have the time, just as we should not wait until we get rich to be generous, for we may never earn a fortune.

Do not wait. We should have the strength to act and the spirit to take charge right now. By not waiting, we have hope of success and a limitless future. When we wait too long, our bodies age and deteriorate, our hair turns gray, while impermanence works its hand and all opportunity is lost! As we wait and wait, the time to plant will pass, the gold will wash away with the river, the sun will set behind the mountains, and the arrows of impermanence will already be aimed at us. Our waiting will only lead us to the master of illusions, the home of failures, the darkness of night, and a life of nothingness.

So, do not wait for things to happen! Take charge of the here and now so we have hope for the future and a life of beauty and benevolence. Do not wait because when life is gone we will be left with nothing but sorrow!

Learn to Admit Mistakes

There is a common shortcoming among politicians and officials-never admitting their mistakes. Actually, this seems to be a common weakness shared by many people. In daily life, when people make mistakes, they often find numerous excuses to cover up their faults.

For instance, some may be half an hour late for a scheduled meeting, but instead of simply offering an apology, they try to excuse their tardiness with all kinds of reasons: traffic jams, last minute calls, unexpected visitors, or even difficulty finding an umbrella for the unexpected rain! There are all sorts of reasons they use to justify their lateness, which they think is no fault of their own. On principle, none of these reasons deserve the empathy of others, because the scheduled meeting time had been agreed upon by everyone concerned and should therefore be adhered to. Whoever is late should admit their fault and simply apologize.

To admit one's mistakes is a virtue! One of the best teachings in Buddhism is to learn to admit one's mistakes. Confucianism teaches, "One should review one's actions three times a day." Moreover, Buddhism actually advocates the scrutiny and repentance of one's body, speech, and mind in every moment. If we are not respectful of our parents, helpful toward our friends, teaching our children well, or contributing sufficiently toward society, we should admit our mistakes.

Daily, when we are late for work, fail to do our jobs well, or when we do not take good enough care of our families, we should recognize our shortcomings. In dealing with others, when we do not return their kindness, when we upset them with inappropriate behavior, or when we wantonly use common resources, we should apologize for our faults.

To admit our faults is to improve ourselves and enhance our morals. In the course of recognizing our mistakes, we learn to review our behavior, which in turn increases our strength. Confucius taught that, "One should not fear correcting one's mistakes." We should, therefore, be brave in admitting our mistakes and correcting them in order to turn over a new leaf in life. There should be no excuses offered with true recognition of our mistakes–simply apologize without hiding behind any screen.

Buddhism advocates "exposure," for being able to expose and repent our faults is a virtue.

In our lifetime, there is much for us to learn–all kinds of knowledge and skills, different ways of getting along with others and handling affairs. Learning to admit our mistakes is an especially important lesson in life for all of us to work on.

Fleeting Enthusiasm

"Fleeting enthusiasm" is used to ridicule a person's lack of determination. It describes someone who does not have the strength to continue what he or she has started, or someone who gives up easily. An alcoholic may swear to stay dry forever, but his or her resolve will dissipate quickly when he or she sees a bottle. People may pledge themselves to worthy causes at the moment of hearing about them, but will soon forget their solemn promise when they move on to something else. Such sudden shift of commitment is a common trait shared by those whose passions and interests only last for a brief period of time.

Human life is full of abrupt changes due to a wide range of emotions. It is like cooking food in the microwave oven, where the dish heats up fast and cools down quickly. It is like planting flowers that bloom and wither in a matter of days. In order for pines and cypresses to grow, the seedlings must endure the change of seasons and withstand the test of time.

Buddhism encourages its practitioners to make a vow of cultivating their bodhi mind. The bodhi mind calls for an unwavering dedication to the learning of Buddhism. However, it is easier to make such a vow than to maintain one's determination in a world that is seductive and delusional. Therefore, the emphasis in learning Buddhism is on non-regression.

In our everyday life, we should care for our parents, especially during times of sickness. We must be patriotic toward our country, especially during times of crisis. "To love one's parents and nation" is not just a slogan, but a practice for life. In starting a business or opening a store, we must be patient when sales are low. We must first concentrate our efforts on establishing good credibility because without a good reputation, our businesses will fail miserably. If we want to make a profit, we must persevere and accept setbacks as matters of course.

Once we make up our mind to liberate all beings from suffering and to pursue perfect enlightenment, we should remain firm in our resolve. Our determination should not be like the morning dew that evaporates when the sun rises. In Buddhism, we have mahasattvas, or "great beings."

They are considered great because they have survived thousands of rebirths and endured eons of incalculable time. They have done what is difficult to do and tolerated what is nearly impossible to bear. Therefore, if our vows are weak and short-lived, we can never attain Buddhahood.

In order to excel in life, we must have the ability to bear prolonged hardships. We must push ourselves ahead by freeing ourselves of unnecessary comforts and persevering through life's bitter challenges. In order to achieve final victory in life, we must keep a low profile and endure all kinds of humiliation. In order to survive in a world of chaos and upheaval, we must persist steadily in our actions and hold firm to our principles.

Some people start projects with a flourish and then work on them in fits and starts, failing to see them through. If a person's enthusiasm is short-lived, he or she will fall short of success for lack of effort. It is like digging a well and leaving the work unfinished right before reaching the water. Therefore, in handling private and public matters, we must endure the tests of time. We must not be frustrated by setbacks and heartbreaking defeats. We must have the ability to experience exertion, pain, or hardship without giving up. We must remain steadfast in our determination and untiring in our struggle. We must make great vows to be relentless and diligent on the long road to enlightenment. As one bodhisattva vow goes, "Although space is finite, I vow to be infinite. Although the world is finite, I vow to be infinite. Although living beings are finite in number, my vow is infinite."

A person's life is not without hardships or failures. In order to have a better future, we must have the stamina and endurance of a marathon runner to carry us past obstacles and difficulties, so we can complete life's course.

Civilization of the Mind

During the Stone Age, when humanity was still uncivilized, people lived in caves, ate raw meat, and covered themselves with leaves or animal skins. Then, they discovered the use of fire and progressed in knowledge over the ages. Now, people use gas and electricity to cook, wear the finest clothes, and live in large houses. This is civilization. However, it is only the civilization of our material lives. We still have to civilize our mind.

What is civilization of the mind? It is when a person progresses from being rude and impolite to being gentle and kind, from being corrupt and immoral to being humble and grateful, and from being selfish and egocentric to caring for others. That is civilization of the mind. When the mind is filled with compassion, wisdom, and wonderful things, the mind becomes civilized. In other words, spiritual reinforcement and mental progress constitute civilization of the mind.

Human nature is basically good. As the sayings go, "Everyone is basically compassionate," or "The original nature of human is kind." Deep within our mind is a civilized world. Buddhism calls it Buddha nature. However, our compassionate Buddha nature has been covered over time with greed, anger, and ignorance and spoiled by materialism and worldly cravings. As a result, we have regressed backwards into barbarism. Often, as our resources increase, our spiritual lives diminish. A country should, therefore, not just pay attention to its material development, but instead, care more about the civilization of the mind of its citizens.

Today, the entire world advocates protection of the environment, purification of the mind, cessation of the nuclear arms race, the promotion of cultural exchanges, and peaceful unification. These are all manifestations of the civilization of the mind. Nowadays, we may find harmony, peace, unity, and friendship in our lives as a result of the cultivation of our mind.

Public organizations and charities care for the aged and young, look after the poor and needy, and provide education. Governments promote openness and efficiency. Medical science is discovering new ways to save lives and relieve suffering caused by disease. These are all advancements of the mind.

Without civilization of the mind, we cannot find joy in our material lives. If the mind is not civilized, then its creations will only be products that kill and threaten the well-being of humanity. How then would it be possible for us to enjoy civilized lives?

How would it be possible to develop values, traditions, religions, languages, philosophy, science, and the arts? When our society becomes more civilized, it progresses. Progress is civilization. The Eastern Pure Land of Crystal Radiance and the Western Pure Land of Ultimate Bliss are both civilized worlds of the mind. The Buddha's Dharma-body (dharmakaya) and Delight-body (sambhogakaya) are also states of civilization. When we can create a beautiful world and a pure land on earth, then we can also enjoy civilization of the mind.

Competing with Ourselves

Life is a marathon with no end to everyone competing for his or her place. Starting from kindergarten and primary school, we compete with other students in schoolwork and exams. Young girls compete with one another to see who is taller or who has a trimmer figure. People compare whose parents are in higher positions and whose houses are bigger. In business, industry, technology, and farming, competition is always present. We can say that in every profession, everyone puts forth one's best effort to compete with others.

It seems like there is competition everywhere! People compete in beauty pageants, singing, and the arts. Between some countries, there is the arms race; and in the Olympics, athletes use their physical prowess to compete for the bronze, silver, and gold medals. According to Darwin's theory of evolution, life is based on survival of the fittest. This highlights the importance of competition.

However, no competition is as important as competing with ourselves! True victory is not overcoming the next person or another country. If we want to compete, we need to conquer ourselves to be the true winners. How do we compete with ourselves? The Chinese scholar Liang Qichao once said, "The 'me' of today is declaring war on the 'me' of yesterday!" Human morals, knowledge, and abilities should always be renewed day after day, since it is with endless creativity, progress, and contribution to humanity that a person can become a victor.

People all have greed, but if we can reduce our greediness, we can prevail over our own obstacles. Furthermore, anger, jealousy, arrogance, and attachments are also shortcomings. If we can rid ourselves of all these unwholesome tendencies, we will triumph over our bad habits and behaviors.

The total grade for the ten lessons of compassion, joyous giving, optimism, progress, diligence, humility, self-contemplation, ethics, selflessness, and righteousness adds up to one hundred. Can we pass the test? How many points can we give ourselves for each of them? If others were to grade us, would we pass? Can we prevail over ourselves?

In history, the Buddha and the saints of other religions were beings who triumphed over themselves, as did all the heroes, sages, and outstanding figures. In conquering ourselves, we overcome personal cravings, attachments, ignorance, and delusion. If we can convert our selfishness, attachment, ignorance, and delusion into selflessness, generosity, wisdom, and enlightenment, then we would have triumphed over ourselves.

Then, wise readers, you can all cheer for and celebrate your ability to triumph over yourselves!

Conquer Ourselves

Soldiers want to conquer their enemy. In marriage, spouses want to dominate each other. Businesspeople wish to conquer their competitors. Big countries wish to conquer small ones, just as the strong are out to conquer the weak. However, even if we do conquer our opponents, we may still be unable to gain control over ourselves.

We need to ask ourselves, "Can we conquer our attachments, selfishness, cravings, and vexations? Can we conquer aging, sickness, and death?" It is easier to conquer others or even the world, but conquering ourselves is as difficult as rising to heaven. Have you ever seen an ordinary individual who has completely mastered his or her own mind?

Throughout history, those who conquered themselves became saints, sages, the virtuous, the benevolent, and the loyal such as the Buddha, bodhisattvas, and arhats. They advocated compassion and selflessness in propagating the Dharma and benefiting all sentient beings. There were people like Gandhi, Confucius, Laozi, Zhuangzi, and Jesus who were able to improve the welfare of humanity with their thinking, teachings, and spirit.

When people are unwilling to correct even minor shortcomings or to change their ways, how can they conquer themselves? It is like arranging furniture on an uneven floor. How would you expect the chairs and tables to be level? As the saying goes, "When we cannot manage a room, how can we rule the nation or the world?"

The first man to climb to the top of Mount Everest, Sir Edmund Hillary, a New Zealander, was asked, "In the process of climbing Everest, what was the biggest challenge?" He replied, "It is not the mountains we conquer but ourselves." It was overcoming and defeating the mental obstacles and stopping his thoughts of giving up.

We cannot conquer the world or others unless we can conquer ourselves. In conquering others, sometimes we use money, physical force, or even love and sex. When we try to control others with these, they can also control us in the same way. However, using compassion, morals and justice to inspire others is the best way to influence others. When they are happily convinced of our integrity and goodwill, they will become our allies. Ultimately, we must first conquer ourselves before we can inspire others.

Conquering the Demon of the Mind

We all fear the demon. However, the demon does not always look vicious and ugly. Sometimes it may appear pretty and lovable.

The demon is not necessarily our enemy. Even though our parents or siblings may obstruct our career for whatever reasons they may have, they are not our enemies. The demon may not necessarily treat us with brutality. It may come in the form of a beautiful woman, alcohol, or narcotics instead of sharp knives or guns. The demon may not be from outside either. For those people who harbor distorted views or hatred against others, the jealousy and anger inside them are demons just the same.

We are often manipulated left and right by our demons. Just like a war, the outer demons conspire with our inner demons in a joint attempt to defeat our achievements and self-respect. The demon is whatever obstructs our mind, thoughts, and resolve in the pursuit of the Dharma. Something may be good-looking or ugly, lovable or repulsive, but as long as it hinders and entraps us, it is the work of the demon.

The trap of money and the temptation of love are common demons. Buddhism considers desire as one of the four demons. This demon has the strength to veil heaven and earth. It challenges our willpower and heart for the Dharma. We should always be on the watch for the victor of the battle.

To put it simply, the demon is none other than our own afflictions. For this reason, we must all be courageous in life because regardless of our status, age, or family background, each of us needs to battle the demon of our afflictions in order to succeed. The demon is not alone either. It has children and even grandchildren, and they all want to ruin our practices with temptations and hurdles.

Before the Buddha attained enlightenment, he first had to subdue the demon, Mara. Throughout history, the virtuous and sages all had to tame their own demons before they fulfilled their accomplishments. In Chinese folklore, there were many demons that posed as lovely beauties and took the lives of numerous scholars who were capable of great achievements. In our own life, we need to overcome demons with benevolence and the power of the demon with the Buddha mind. We must view the demon's world with the eyes of wisdom and, with diligence, rid ourselves of afflictions and obstructions.

We cannot always clearly distinguish the good from the bad of the world on our own. We must use religion, sutras, and the Buddha's teachings in order to thoroughly understand the world of the demon. We must use the strength of concentration, wisdom, and faith in order to subdue the demon.

Where is the demon? It is not far away; the demon is right here beside us.

Intentions

How do we make progress in this world? We must, at least, have the intention of bettering ourselves. We must, at least, be willing to make vows. In order to be wise and virtuous, we must first have the intention to be wise and virtuous. In order to better our society, we must first have the determination to help others.

It is very important that our intentions are wholesome instead of shameless plotting. They must not come from the need to seek advantages for ourselves. If our intentions are not pure and altruistic, they can lead to crime. Therefore, we must direct the purpose of what we plan to do toward the good of humanity. We must keep in mind that good intentions give us the motivation to accomplish that which is philanthropic and beautiful.

In this world, there are those who are willing to put forth all their time and effort to bring benefits to their communities. There are also those who are willing to lay down their lives for justice and righteousness. On the other hand, we have often been disappointed by the misconduct of government officials. Most of us have also been cheated or swindled at one time or another. In fact, it has become a common occurrence in today's society to see someone who will unscrupulously seek pleasure at another's expense, or take every shortcut available with the hope of hitting the jackpot. Unlike the days of our forefathers, people no longer believe in the fruit of labor. They have become susceptible to any scheme that promises a fast track to fame and fortune. Therefore, in comparing the deeds of a person who is virtuous and a person who is not, the intentions become apparent. The virtuous person will always plan to benefit others, while the other will always do the opposite.

If we want to accomplish something worthwhile or important, intention alone is not enough. We must first have the resolve to do something great, and then we must take the necessary steps to translate our goals into actions. People whose achievements have gone down in history all had great ambition and determination. Every one of them had the aspiration to change the world and the course of history forever. Without a strong desire to achieve greatness, none of them would be remembered by later generations. Because of their intentions and their willingness for action, they achieved unparalleled distinctions and honors. Not every successful person in this world is born with a silver spoon in his or her mouth. On the road to fame and fortune, most of these people had to overcome adversities and obstacles. We should, indeed, follow their examples in whatever we do, first setting our sight on something that is worthwhile and significant, and then putting forth all our effort towards realizing our goals.

What should we fear most in life? We should be fearful of laziness and passivity. We should be fearful of indolence and moral degeneration. We should be fearful of inaction and cowardice. We should be most fearful of not accomplishing anything in our lifetimes. What we must have is the ambition to achieve greatness. We must be people of virtue and principle. We must have the intention to attain enlightenment here and now, or our lives will be wasted.

Increasing Capacity

Through much technological research and innovation, airplanes can now fly at higher altitudes, with greater capacity, and for longer distances. Cars can have a range of engine capacity, such as 1200cc, 2400cc, and 3600cc. Fleet horses can travel hundreds of miles a day, and elephants can carry heavy loads because of their strength. But, how much can people carry?

People can carry heavy loads as well. For instance, we have to pay family expenses, support our parents, provide for our children's education, and pay for medical, travel, and social activities. In addition, there are personal worries, troubles, frustrations, worldly affairs, human rights, and all kinds of concerns. These things are heavy enough to crush us, but we still need to summon the strength to carry on. Like an old ox dragging a cart, we are loaded time and again with all kinds of pressures, but we keep moving on with all our might. Our personal loads of glory and shame, good and bad fortune, gain and loss can all be very heavy, creating much toil for us. Therefore, we have no choice but to train ourselves to increase our capacity in order to shoulder life's many tastes and be able to bear all of its honor and abuse.

How do we increase our capacity? We study, train, practice, and discipline ourselves to increase our capacity. Other people can only help us a little. Causes and conditions can also provide us with some assistance, so we should seize them whenever and wherever we can. When we are faced with a wide range of circumstances, we need to rely on ourselves to develop the strength to deal with various situations. We cannot count on the help of external forces from heaven, earth, or other people. They may not come through for us, so blaming them will not resolve our problems.

Buddhist sutras indicate that strength comes in five ways: faith, diligence, right mindfulness, concentration, and wisdom. Faith is strength! In climbing a mountain, no matter how high it is, nor how much we sweat and gasp on the way up, we will not be defeated because our faith motivates us.

With diligence, we will work hard and not give any excuses to delay work. We will not be lazy and idle. Instead, we will rise to the occasion, and the strength from our diligence will give us energy and enable us to carry our own load.

Right mindfulness is right thoughts, right thinking, and right understanding. As the saying goes, "Deviance cannot overcome righteousness." Nor can confusion, indolence, or complexity overcome right mindfulness.

Concentration brings self-assurance. With concentration, we will remain unmoved in the face of money or sex, staying as calm and clear as a still pond. We will be able to see clearly through right and wrong, gain and loss in the world.

Wisdom is especially important in life. Some people may toil for a year and achieve very little, while the words of wisdom of another may bring him or her endless wealth. Therefore, we need to develop the wisdom to guide our emotions, thoughts, and the work we do.

Faith, diligence, right mindfulness, concentration, and wisdom are indeed within our capacity!

In war, whoever has the most power wins the battle. In the case of a love triangle, whoever is more attractive and charming gains love. In business, the one with the most capital gains business opportunities. In human relations, the ones who have the greatest capacity in their hearts, and the most wisdom, are the winners in life.

Winning Awards

When applause for the winner of an award is heard, the winner's efforts, energy, and strife are rewarded. As the saying goes, "Remain anonymous for a decade in one's endeavors, become world-renowned overnight for one's success." After diligent cultivation over time, at harvest, the fruits of success taste particularly sweet. To be given an award is certainly a form of recognition and honor. There are some well-known awards in society: the renowned Nobel Prize, the MacArthur Award, the Oscar, and the highest honor in journalism, the Pulitzer Prize. The announcements of these awards are always eagerly anticipated by the public each year.

In Taiwan too, there are a number of awards every year to honor exemplary people in their professions. There are awards for teachers, farmers, and soldiers, as well as for outstanding young people, mothers and fathers, and those serving in various social services. The entertainment industry gives out different awards to actors, musicians, and artists. There are also awards for books and even food products. The great number of awards is a sure indication that the different professions and businesses in society are flourishing.

Giving awards as recognition and encouragement has been a practice since ancient times. Ancient kings and emperors would bestow plaques, gifts, or promotions upon meritorious subjects. Nowadays, there are monetary prizes, trophies, cups, and medals. These awards represent the countless efforts and accomplishments of the recipients.

However, the process of winning awards may not necessarily be fair. Given a certain profession, there may be some who are more outstanding in their accomplishments than the award-winners, but whose high achievements remain undiscovered. Or, in a nomination for a particular award, the judges may hold different criteria, thus forfeiting those who may be just as deserving as the winner. Therefore, after every contest, we should certainly applaud the winners, but we should also root for the other contestants to encourage them to strive on. Even for those who may not have the chance to compete, we should show our care and explore their potential so no talent is lost.

The government of Taiwan encourages its citizens to nominate candidates every year for outstanding contributions to social causes. As a result, some who are not qualified try every means possible to be nominated, while those who are most deserving keep a low profile out of self-respect and aversion to fame. Therefore, we should realize that in addition to those who win awards, there are still others who are more honorable, who have more integrity, and who quietly contribute in different areas of the community. They do not seek fame or applause from the public. In fact, they are the ones who are more deserving of a recognition or award.

As the Chinese saying goes, "There are some who rush all night to the capital for the imperial examination, and then there are those who resign their positions overnight to return to their hometowns." This illustrates the differences in human nature that exist in the world. Regardless of how others behave, we should realize that there are causes and conditions for winning awards, so we should not be discouraged if we do not win. As long as we cultivate positive and wholesome causes and conditions, there will come a time when we will be well-qualified to win an award.

Do Not Belittle One's Own Value

How much does a person weigh? It is probably somewhere between one and three hundred pounds. However, while one's body weight is measurable, one's character is immeasurable.

A person's weight should not be measured in kilograms or pounds; it should be assessed according to moral character and wisdom. In evaluating a person's contribution to his or her family or society in general, only those who know him or her best are able to pass judgments. Any recognizable achievement must withstand the test of time. Self-glorification is not an acceptable standard for evaluating one's worth.

Some of us must work very hard for a dollar, while others can give away millions on a whim. Is it really appropriate to measure one's value by how much one earns? Some people will do anything for the sake of obtaining high positions or high-paying jobs, while others will avoid any opportunity for fame or fortune. From one's actions and intentions, we can readily tell if one has high moral standards or not.

A person's character is worth more than anything in the world. A person of high integrity will not abandon his or her principles when lured by wealth or position. They cannot be bought with money or power. When faced with the possibility of death, Socrates was unwilling to escape prison to live a life in exile. Instead, he was ready to die for the sake of preserving his integrity and beliefs. Past Chan masters had only one goal, that of enlightenment. Attaining Buddhahood or becoming the patriarch of a certain practice was not the achievement they sought. On the contrary, people today have forgotten the meaning of "blood is thicker than water" in a family when fighting over money. Brothers and sisters turn against each other in order to obtain a bigger portion of their family estate or they even go to court to secure their shares. Fortunately, there are still those who value family unity more than money. They would rather keep silent and forsake their rights in order to keep their families happy and together. Through cases like these, we can judge whether family or money is more important to a person.

In ancient China, it was customary for a man to pay a dowry to secure a promise of marriage. As long as he was willing to pay the right price, he could have more than one wife. Where is the dignity in this old practice of buying a bride or a concubine? Can we really put a price tag on surrendering one's pride and self-respect? Some people would rather starve themselves than to take food from their enemies. Some people would never give in to unwholesome behavior even in the face of adversity and hardship. Some would rather remain poor and moral than wealthy and immoral. Therefore, in the face of poverty and misery, a person's integrity and moral character becomes easily evident.

Su Dongpo, a famous poet of the Song Dynasty, was very proud of his literary achievements. One of his passions was to challenge virtuous elders of his day to difficult debates. One time, when he visited Chan Master Yuquan, he disguised himself as a high court official in order to test the Chan Master's grasp of the Buddha's teachings. Upon receiving him, the Chan Master respectfully asked for his name. The poet replied, "My name is Scale, and my job is to weigh the value of all virtuous elders." Instead of saying anything, Chan Master Yuquan let out a loud shout and asked, "How much does this shout weigh?" The poet was rendered speechless and was immediately convinced of the Chan Master's wisdom.

As stated in the *Confucian Analects*, "If a man of virtue does not have self-respect, he will not be an imposing figure." We must, therefore, be disciplined in our words and deeds. We must have self-esteem in conducting ourselves and have self-respect every second of our lives. If we do not have confidence in our own merit as an individual, and if we do not firmly believe in our own worth and dignity, we cannot expect others to have any respect for us. "With too much self-reproach, others will impart their criticisms; with too much self-contempt, others will convey their disrespect." Therefore, to establish ourselves as worthy people and to get along with others, we must rid ourselves of arrogance, and more importantly, self-contempt.

Going Upstream

As the saying goes, "Learning is like rowing upstream, we go backwards if we stop our progress." In learning a foreign language, we can easily regress if we do not practice it often. Similarly, in our studies, if we do not keep up with them, we will not progress. Life always feels like "going upstream," for without diligence and effort we will regress. The first stage of attainment in arhathood means "upstream"–going against the stream of life and death to gain liberation. The gushing stream of life and death allows no opportunity for us to stop. If we do not progress, we will fall back.

Nowadays, there are many who strive for a career, but once they are faced with setbacks or obstacles they give up. Just as the current in the ocean does not allow us to stop our journey for a moment, once we stop trying others will overtake us. So, if we do not summon our will to press on, we will either be swallowed by the raging waves or crippled by their power, unable to get up on our feet again.

In a business partnership, if either partner only wishes to share the profits and not the hard work, once the capital is gone, the business will dissolve. To stay in the mainstream business world, we need to invest and increase our capital, so we can overcome the challenge of going upstream and withstand the tests of time and space to achieve success. Even in a small business, it is a fantasy to expect a profit within a few months after the opening of the shop. When going upstream in the business world, a new business must struggle for a few years before it can make a profit.

In today's society, there are many socio-economic levels. Many successful people experienced endless adversities and setbacks before reaching their social position, like a butterfly that finally struggled out of its cocoon. To strive for success is like going upstream: no pain, no gain. If we lack this type of resilience, merely relying on taking advantage of others and not doing our parts, then we have to be content to remain downstream.

Scholars may spend decades in their studies before they gain success in their endeavors, just as a fruit tree may take ten years before bearing rich and bountiful fruit. In every profession, perseverance and hard work are needed for achievement. Like a tower made of grains of sand, we all need to strive upstream in the ocean of humanity before we can reach the land of success.

In going against the current of life, we must make every effort to progress; in negotiating the upstream journey of life and death, we must work hard to move forward. To advance our careers, we must swim up the stream of competition to strengthen ourselves to be successful. In the ocean of knowledge, scholars must break through the wind and waves with a spirit of determination in order to succeed in their fields. As practitioners, as long as we have the spirit to go upstream, then we will eventually attain Buddhahood.

Building a Good Foundation

Many people in society today share the bad habit of not caring enough about establishing good foundations for themselves. In building tall buildings, an unsound foundation can cause a collapse. In building bridges, an unsafe foundation can lead to disaster. In the same manner, highways can go to wreck and gullies can become clogged. Because the quality of foundation work cannot be easily determined, an insufficient base can often be overlooked if what is visible appears to be in order. Therefore, there is a prevalence of carelessness and superficiality in society. A good foundation is generally lacking in almost every undertaking.

Students only care about moving up to the next grade. They do not bother to establish a good foundation in their studies. In business, people do not build a solid foundation regarding their capital, facilities, material, and clientele. Without a good foundation, their business ventures fold as quickly as they start. Lovers do not concern themselves with the foundation of their love. All they care about is external good looks and sweet talk; taking love at first sight as their basis, they decide to spend their lives together. They pay no attention to whether they are compatible with each other's habits, ideals, faith, or morals. Because of the lack of a solid foundation in their relationship, they often experience problems. Just like a flower planted in sand, their relationship cannot withstand the elements.

In today's world, the outlook is not all rosy. Many problems arise because of the lack of good foundations in society. In politics, we witness bribery, vote rigging, partisan bickering, and scandals. In the economy, we see massive speculation, defaults, scams, and frauds. As for the environment, we face blatant destruction of the land, forests, rivers, and the air, not to mention the ongoing threat to endangered species. There is total disregard for public health and safety. The general public ought to be educated on the importance of such issues.

We must pay close attention to the state of affairs in the world. It is imperative that we build good foundations for the economy, in international relationships, in our faith, and more importantly, in ethics and morals. We need to inform all global citizens about the benefits to be gained in building a good foundation. Without us allowing a solid foundation to take root in our endeavors, it will be impossible to grow and develop a sturdy trunk.

Projects of Hope

In China and Taiwan nowadays, it is common to consider education for children and any related business as "projects of hope." For instance, in building an elementary school in some remote village, we tell others we are contributing toward a "project of hope." In publishing children's books, we also say we are involved in a "project of hope."

"Projects of hope" is a popular term these days; many people seem to think that it is a new invention. Since ancient times, all matters that benefit humanity and society have been "projects of hope." When a country builds a new highway to improve transportation, is it not a project of hope? Is increasing the availability of air and water transportation not a project of hope? Endeavors that improve the quality of life for people such as building a park to enhance greenery in the environment or establishing a library to encourage the cultivation of wisdom are also projects of hope. In building a new community, the emphasis placed on humanity and culture is another project of hope. Reforestation and efforts to protect the environment are projects of hope as well. Essentially, if everyone takes the initiative to work for the benefit of society, then every person is contributing to a project of hope.

Everyone's physical body is a project in and of itself. By paying attention to nutrition, exercising daily, walking properly, and even breathing, we are working on our healthy body project. Even in our daily meditation and cultivation we are working on two projects: our mental and physical health. When our personal mental and physical projects are in good shape, we benefit ourselves and others, as well as the whole community. So, every person's individual project of hope is also society's project of hope.

Children are projects of hope for a family. The trees and flowers outside the house are projects of hope for the entire household. People live in hope. Without taking part in projects of hope, where can we find hope? In daily life, our mind encounters much right and wrong, good and bad; being willing to reflect on ourselves is a way to fortify our mind–this is another project of hope. In life, there is this and that, here and there; in time, there is this year and the next. When we live in hope, our lives will be filled with numerous opportunities and our days will be full of endless benefits.

A Moment, A Lifetime

Some things last only a moment, others last a lifetime. Feeling moved lasts for a moment, but gratitude is for a lifetime. Glory is for a moment, but the inspiration is for a lifetime. Upholding the precepts takes a moment, but upholding them is for a lifetime. Being wronged lasts for a moment, but achievement is for a lifetime.

A moment or a lifetime, which is longer? Most people naturally think that a moment is very short and a lifetime very long. In fact, eons exist in a ksana, a moment of time. Hence, even though it is a mere moment, is it not also a lifetime?

Dharma practitioners are diligent in their efforts with no fear for difficulties or setbacks. Their hard work is for the moment only, but the Dharma joy upon enlightenment is eternal. Many people like to fight and compete, and often, unable to bear a moment of anger or hate, they end up causing immeasurable damage to themselves and others. Likewise, losing control of one's temper for a moment results in endless regret.

Sometimes we may say something unintentionally, but as the saying goes, "A word can make or break a nation." A few words can destroy someone or allow a person to make a comeback from a seemingly desperate situation. A single utterance can determine good or bad, life or death for a person. While it only takes a moment to say a few words, the damage done can last a long time. How can we thus not be cautious with what we say?

Today's young people are often hot-blooded. In a show of bravado, they enjoy racing each other at very high speeds on roads and highways. However, the high they get from speeding lasts only a moment, but they may sustain a lifelong injury. Is it really worth it?

The time students spend in school studying diligently lasts momentarily, while their achievements can last them a lifetime. Those who have a high understanding of cultivation are willing to toil for the moment in exchange for the best in life. The wedding ceremony for a bride and groom may last a moment, but their coexistence is shared over a lifetime. To maintain a lifetime of shared happiness, neither should forget the commitment they made to each other at that moment. In a democratic election, voters can only cast one vote; however, the influence of the elected official is far-reaching and the effect of the policies he or she makes can be immense.

A moment passes very quickly, but a lifetime lasts long into the future. Even in the most difficult of situations, if we can remember it is only momentary, then we can overcome any hardship or setback. On the other hand, even during the greatest moment of enjoyment, we should also remind ourselves that it is only momentary so that we will not become attached and crave for more. For those who are attached to neither suffering or joy, there is nothing they cannot achieve.

We should tell ourselves that in anything we do, benefiting others is for a lifetime, and hard work is only for a moment. With this in mind, we will persevere and persist in our efforts. During the course of our life, the causes we plant in the moment may affect our fortune and well-being in our many lifetimes to come. Therefore, how can we not be cautious with what we say and do at each moment? For the sake of this lifetime and the many lifetimes to come, we must pay careful attention to the effect a moment may have in anything we do.

Learning to Adapt and Let Go

"The ability to adapt and the willingness to let go" are very important in determining a person's success or failure. In recent Chinese history, both Chiang Kai-shek and Deng Xiaoping learned this lesson well. If they had failed to recognize their situations, they would not have succeeded in implementing reforms for their countries' economies. Mao Zedong of the Chinese Communist Party also understood the importance of adaptability when he overcame early alienation from his own party to become its most powerful and feared leader. As for those who did not learn to let go as the occasion demanded, they often encountered tragedies.

What does it mean to "adapt and let go"? It is like drawing water out of a well, being able to lift up the water bucket but also being able to lower it down again. However, many people today lack the ability to overcome setbacks and adversities. When things do not go their way, they cannot let go, and they fail to adapt. Politicians, entertainers, business-people, students, and ordinary citizens are often victims of their own frustration. Worse yet, some of them even contemplate suicide as a solution to their problems, because they are too rigid in their ways of thinking and are unable to see the light at the end of the tunnel.

During the Buddha's time, a Brahman visited the Buddha with two vases. When the Buddha saw him, he asked the Brahman to "let go." Complying with the Buddha's request, the Brahman put down the vases, but the Buddha again asked him to "let go." Confused by the Buddha's words, the Brahman asked, "I have done what you have told me. What else do you want me to put down?"

The Buddha replied, "I did not mean for you to put down the vases, but to let go of your bad intentions and negative emotions, such as arrogance, pride, jealousy, and hatred."

While it is not easy for one to renounce his or her worldly possessions and honors, it is even harder for someone to let go of his or her emotions. It is only through cultivating the virtue of modesty and practicing self-reflection can one truly appreciate the meaning of "in retreating, one advances; in letting go, one adapts." During the Cultural Revolution in

China, teachers were publicly humiliated and party leaders were banished to hard labor camps. While some did not survive the harsh treatment, others lived to see the end of the nightmare, because they were flexible and adaptable.

"Let go of your status" is a popular saying in today's society because in this ever-changing world of ours, "no flower can bloom for a hundred days, and no one can stay well for a thousand days." Adaptability will only be possible if we are willing to let go of our ego and be modest. For example, Puyi, the last emperor of China, would not have survived if he did not learn to forsake the prestige of the imperial throne and be content with his life as a groundskeeper at a park in Beijing.

How then should we conduct ourselves in life? We should be like a piece of luggage that can be picked up when necessary and set down when not. Everyone likes to pursue fame and fortune, and there is nothing wrong with this, especially when they can be used to benefit others. However, when fame and fortune are lost due to circumstances, we should learn to let go.

In our lives, if we are to be successful, we must learn to adapt. We must be flexible and broad-minded in the face of success or failure, having or not having, or being outstanding or ordinary. We will not be troubled by any positive or negative circumstance once we have the ability to advance and the willingness to retreat as the situation demands.

The Past, the Present, and the Future

In life, there is past, present, and future. In a broader sense, countless kalpas consist in the past, numerous kalpas are in the future, and the present is the time from birth to death. Although we do not specifically know our past lives and what we did then, to know the present, we can still look to the past; history can teach us many lessons. Likewise, we do not know what is in store for us in the future. Whether we will meet good or bad fortune, we have no way of knowing at present; we can only look to the past for hints of the future.

Our lives of the present also include the past and the future. Everything that happened before today is now a part of our past. Everything that comes after today is our future. When we reflect on the days before today–how our parents nurtured us, how our teachers taught us, and how others in the community gave us good causes and conditions–we can see how we have grown and matured amidst the benefits that others have bestowed on us. Though at times we may have thought of how we should repay them for their generosity, yet due to our selfishness and attachments, many of us have not really cared for those who nurtured, taught, and benefited us in the past with earnestness and devotion. For this reason, we are deeply remorseful about our past.

When we look at the future from the present, we do not have a clue as to what it will hold. It is only natural for us all to hope that, for the sake of our future fields of merit, seeds can be widely planted for wonderful fruit and flowers. Then, we will lack nothing in life. When we are able to plant the seedlings of merit in the fields of our future, we will be able to harvest a bumper crop, and our lives will be full. However, our present resources for merit are insufficient. We are unable to plant seeds in the "field of eight merits" as we should. Our past has directly influenced our present. But the past is already beyond our reach; we cannot undo anything in the past, but we can prepare for the future right now. We have to take control of the present to prepare. So how do we prepare for the future?

First of all, we should refrain from killing, stealing, and engaging in sexual misconduct in order to cultivate wholesome physical behaviors. Secondly, we should refrain from harsh speech, flattery, being forked-tongued, and lying in order to practice good speech. Thirdly, we should give instead of covet, be compassionate instead of malevolent, and be rational instead of holding deviant views.

As the saying goes, "If one wants to know the causes from previous lives, they are manifested in this life. If one wants to know the effect in future lives, they are being caused in this life." We need to "eradicate past unwholesome karma as the circumstances arise, and not create new ones." As long as we cultivate diligently in the present, planting positive and benevolent seeds, we need not fear the lack of a good harvest in the future.

From the Past to the Future

We all have a past, a present, and a future. There are people who like to think of the past and hold on to fond memories, saying it is better than the present. Some people like to make use of the present. With both their feet on the ground, they believe that the present is most important. Others like to hope for the future, thinking that there is no need to rush now because there is always the future. Which is more important? Our time goes from past to present to future. However, what is past is past, no matter how wonderful and glorious it might have been. So what is the point of living in the past?

Once, a woman had a twelve year old son who suddenly got sick and died. The woman was overcome with grief and went from house to house crying over his death. She eventually went to the Buddha with the hope that he could bring her son back to life. The Buddha asked her to get a stalk of "auspicious grass" from a house where no one had ever died, and she would be able to save her son. The woman looked for a few days but could not find a household where no one had ever died. Naturally, she could not find such grass. Eventually, she understood the Buddha's message and was comforted.

We should realize that impermanence is the truth of life! If we become attached to immortality, then we fail to understand the truth. The desire to hold onto the past forever is a form of attachment. We should know that the past leads to the present, the present is in the future, and the future will become the past, forming the cycle of the three time periods.

The *Sutra on Cause and Effect of the Three Time Periods* states, "If one wants to know the causes of the past life, just look at what one experiences in this lifetime. If one wants to know the effects of a future life, they are created in this lifetime." In reality, what is past is not really past as it also affects our present. The present will not stop as it leads us into the future and the future of the future. Life continues in the cycle of birth and death.

We should reflect on our past behavior and learn from our mistakes in order to improve in the future. We should not stop where we are and close ourselves off, because if we do not give up where we have been, how can we move on? It is important that we motivate ourselves to progress toward benevolence and truth. Being able to make use of the present moment to cultivate our morals and behavior will bring us a beautiful future.

In reality, the past, present, and future are all ours as the three time periods are all here and now in our mind. We need to make good use of the past, present, and future so that we can circulate and sustain benevolent actions and thoughts, and we can live fulfilled lives.

Whatever contributions our ancestors made to benefit society, we should exalt. Moreover, whatever harm they may have caused to society or others, we should make up for it. We should work to purify and beautify the stream of life from the past to the present and to the future. What we are doing now will surely affect our future and even that of our children and grandchildren. We should cultivate morals and good causes and conditions for future generations. This is a way of extending our lifeline.

Even if we are unable to create an endless lifeline for our country and society, we should leave some good causes and conditions for our own families. It is important not to be attached to the past, not to be reluctant to part with the present, and not to fantasize about the future. In dealing with the past, present, and future of life, we just need to be responsible and do our best!

Black Mouse, White Mouse

The following story comes from a Buddhist sutra: There was once a traveler walking in the wilderness. All of a sudden, he saw a huge elephant running toward him. Out of fear, he ran for cover, but there was nowhere to hide. Finally, he saw a dry well, so he climbed into it by holding on to hanging vines. Just as he was about to reach the bottom, he saw that there were four large snakes. Afraid to let go, he hung on to the vines tightly. Looking up, he noticed a black mouse and a white mouse gnawing at the vines. At this critical moment, five honeybees flew by the well and dropped five drops of honey right into the mouth of the traveler. Upon tasting the sweetness of the honey, the traveler forgot about the danger he was in.

What is the meaning of this story? The elephant represents the impermanence of time that is always chasing us. We seek for cover in the dry well, which symbolizes the abyss of the cycle of life and death. The four snakes at the bottom are the four elements of our bodies: earth, water, fire, and wind. These four elements depend on the lifeline of the vine, which helps sustain us for the time being. However, the black mouse and the white mouse by the side of the well represent day and night, which are slowly but steadily gnawing away at the vines. The five drops of honey from the bees are the five sensual desires of wealth, beauty, fame, food, and sleep. Upon tasting the sweetness, the traveler forgets about the imminent dangers.

There is an old Chinese saying, "Time shoots by like an arrow as the day and night go by like a weaver's shuttle." Our lives gradually move toward impermanence, between the black mouse and the white mouse of day and night.

Impermanence is one of the truths in Buddhism. Of all the phenomena in the world, which one of them is not controlled by impermanence? Life is impermanent, as is the earth, its mountains and its rivers. Due to their impermanent nature, things can change for the better; but more often than not, they change for the worse! The impermanence of the days of our lives is like the deposits in our bank accounts. They shrink by the day and lessen by the year. When the deposits are all used up, our lives all hang in the balance of the mercy of the black and the white mouse.

Due to this impermanence of life, we must make the best use of time. We should finish what we need to do and not take unfinished aspirations to the grave with us. Life is very precious, but time is even more valuable. Human life is difficult to come by, and time never returns. So what should we leave for the world? Even though the black mouse and the white mouse gnaw at our lives continuously, we should make full use of the time we have and do what needs to be done. For instance, we should ask ourselves, "What have we done to benefit others? Have we borne our share of responsibilities for our families? What have we left behind in the world for others to cherish?" Though the two mice might have bitten off the vines of our lifeline, our spirit and merits can be passed on to society or at least remain in the hearts of relatives and friends.

Each person should have strength in life. In a moment, we are capable of completing work that can last for years to come. As long as we have the determination and efficiency to do so, why fear the black mouse and the white mouse?

The Truth of Impermanence

"People do not enjoy a thousand good days in a row, and flowers do not stay in bloom for a hundred days." This is an illustration of impermanence. "The moon waxes and wanes from month to month, just as people's fortunes ebb and flow from day to day." This also expresses the meaning of impermanence.

Impermanence means change and movement. It applies to people, plants, trees, animals, and all things. It is not affected by power, and it does not discriminate. Because of its universal nature, impermanence has been proven as the truth or principle of all sentient and non-sentient things.

There are many beautiful things in the world, but because of impermanence, they do not last. Youth and beauty do not exist forever; fame, power, and money come and go. According to science, even the cells of our bodies are constantly changing. So, the past "me" is not the same "me" of today. The "me" of today will not be the same "me" of tomorrow. There are endless changes; all lives and things are impermanent!

Impermanence is not a truth that has to inspire pessimism. Because of impermanence, where there was formerly nothing, something new can happen. There are many examples to illustrate this idea. We might be poor, but with the right causes and conditions on top of our great effort, we can become wealthy. We may lack schooling, but if we work hard and apply ourselves, we can become educated and gain knowledge and skills. We may be childless at first, but in time we may still end up with a family of many children. Land may be vacant, but with a good design, the proper materials, and the teamwork of architects, engineers, contractors, and skilled workers, tall buildings can be constructed. "Wondrous things come into being from emptiness." Is this not also an aspect of impermanence?

Impermanence is not to be feared, nor is it avoidable. Regrettably, some people are terrified of impermanence. They fool themselves by thinking that if they avoid it, they will not be affected by its ever-changing nature. However, there is no escape from impermanence.

When we watch flowers bloom and wither, are we not alarmed by their impermanence? In witnessing births and deaths, have we come to understand the phenomena of living and dying? We not only should learn to embrace impermanence; we should even see our future in impermanence. We should complete whatever job needs to be done and pursue our goals so that when impermanence manifests itself, we will not be left with unfulfilled wishes, broken promises, or regrets.

Impermanence is truly wonderful! As the saying goes, "The good will come when the bad leaves." Impermanence can bring pain and sorrow, especially in sickness and aging, but the renewal that impermanence brings is joyous and celebrated. We can transform bad into good, just as we can transcend impermanence and enter into the permanent dharma realms of suchness.

To Cherish One's Body

"It is difficult to be born in the human realm; likewise, it is a rare opportunity to hear the Dharma." Buddhism teaches that the opportunity to attain a human body is as miniscule as a handful of soil and the chance of losing it is as great as all the soil on earth. An analogy in the *Lotus Sutra* illustrates the rarity of attaining a human body as follows: A blind tortoise wanted to float on the ocean surface, but it needed the help of a floating log to do so; yet, the chance of a blind turtle finding one in the vast ocean is very small.

Since it is as difficult to attain a human body as it is for a blind turtle to find a floating log in the vast ocean, we should take good care of it. If we get sick or are injured, our families will be burdened physically and financially in caring for us. However, some do not cherish themselves and may even destroy their bodies by committing suicide.

The body is not simply for eating and sleeping; otherwise, it would be no different than a piece of furniture or a rice pot. Over pampering the body and allowing it to become slothful is of course wrong, but not giving it proper rest and nourishment is also not right. We should use our bodies to serve our families and the community. If we engage our healthy bodies in rightful endeavors and contribute to society, the value of our human bodies will be enhanced. When a tree provides cool shade for the traveler, it is cherished. Similarly, when a bridge allows people to cross over water, it is valued. In cherishing the human body, should we not be like the shady tree or the bridge in benefiting others?

In the Buddha's time, there was a practitioner who had the supernatural power of clairvoyance. One day, he saw someone whipping a corpse by the roadside. In his curiosity, he went up and asked, "He is already dead, why whip his body?"

The person replied, "What do you know? This body is my previous life who committed all sorts of evil deeds when it was alive. Now I suffer in hell for his acts. So I can only get back at him by whipping it!"

As he went on his way, the practitioner saw another person worshipping a corpse with flowers and incense. Again he asked, "Since he is already dead, do you really need to worship him with offerings of incense and flowers?"

The person explained, "Oh, you do not understand. This body is my previous life. When he was alive, he was compassionate and benevolent, respectful of the Triple Gem, practiced filial piety, and benefited his community with his kindness. Because of him, I am now reborn in heaven and enjoy a life of good fortune and happiness. In order to express my gratitude, I am here to worship him!"

The human body is not only closely related to us in this lifetime, it also affects our future lives. Should we not cherish it well?

Karmic Power and Vows

The *Sutra of the Ksitigarbha Bodhisattva* states, "What kind of people enter hell? That is determined by either their unwholesome karma or the strengths of their vows." In order for one to go to heaven, it takes wholesome karma or the strength of one's vows. As humans transmigrate between the six realms of existence or attain arhatship, they all depend on the power of karma and vows.

Karma is sometimes out of our control. Due to various past causes and conditions, we are drawn into creating much wholesome or unwholesome karma in the course of our daily lives. For instance, unwholesome karma is acquired when we kill, steal, or engage in sexual misconduct; when we lie, speak harshly, deceive others, or engage in senseless talk; and when we are greedy, deluded, or hold deviant views.

When we acquire unwholesome karma, we will reap its fruit. No one, including our families or even our own selves, can aid us; not even Buddhas or bodhisattvas can aid us. Similarly, when we have done good deeds, without the need for any special assistance from others, we will naturally enjoy the positive results.

If, unfortunately, we have built up unwholesome karma, we can address it in the following ways:

1. We need to cleanse it. When dirt gets on our clothes or bodies, we can use detergent or soap to wash it off. When we have acquired unwholesome karma, we must repent in order to cleanse ourselves of karmic obstruction.
2. We need to increase the strength of our vows by vowing to do good deeds, to fill our mind with good thoughts, and to speak good words. In addition to making these vows, we must put them into action so they will be realized.

In looking at history, those who were rich and powerful could be toppled overnight when their past unwholesome karmic power manifested itself. On the other hand, those who were in dire poverty could accomplish anything they wished for when their good causes and conditions worked together in their favor. Tyrants might reign with glory in their heyday, but were still overthrown when the time came, and they became history. On the other hand, average citizens, farmers, or workers could rise to the occasion and become rulers of the land when the causes and conditions were right.

The circumstances in life are like the highs and lows on a road. The pathway can be smooth and straight or winding and bumpy. Our circumstances are determined by the unwholesome and unwholesome karma we have acquired. If we want to rid ourselves of unwholesome karma, we should first do more good deeds. By planting good seeds in a fertile field, we will not fear the lack of a harvest. When we always have kind thoughts, make vows to take positive actions, and actually practice them by being loyal to our country, benefiting the community, respecting our parents, and helping our friends and neighbors, we will succeed in anything we set out to do. By keeping such positive vows in our mind all the time, the vows will surely be realized.

The greatest strength in the world is not that of gushing water or vicious animals, nor is it that of bombs or bullets. In reality, the happiness and misery of the world all hinge on karmic power and vows. How can we not be cautious in what we say or do? How can we not strive to rid ourselves of unwholesome karma, resolve our worries, and embrace great vows to help others?

I Am a Part of It All

Let me take part in doing good deeds. Let me make connections with good people. Let me share in all good things. How wonderful life is when I can share in all of these!

In reality, there is nothing in this world that we do not share. We are part of the earth, our nation, mountains, rivers, parks, roads, and even the airports and harbors. Even though I may not be able to afford to live in the building you built, I can still use its archway as a shelter from the rain. I can shop at the department store you own. I can work in the factory you operate. I can enjoy the beauty of flowers and trees you planted. I can share in your family celebrations. I am a part of everything!

When you open a bank, I can have a savings account there. If you publish a newspaper, I can be your subscriber. If you make air-conditioners, refrigerators, or engines, my life can be more comfortable. If you are a car dealer, I could buy a car from you and travel anywhere at will. If you write a book, I can be your reader. If you give a speech, I can be your audience. Moreover, there are things I can share in nature: luminous moonlight, soft breezes, high mountains, and flowing rivers. None of the fortune and infrastructure of this world needs to be mine, but I can appreciate them all the same. No one can take the enjoyment away from me. Therefore, as long as we want to, we can be a part of anything in this world and not be lacking in any way.

We have to improve environmental protection and the preservation of the ecosystem, because it is our earth, and we are part of it. This is my country, and I am willing to make sacrifices for it. For this reason, if others transgress on my country's sovereignty, I will be willing to defend it with my life when necessary. The family is mine and so is the community. All people are my siblings and I, therefore, view them as wonderful. I cannot love them enough. How is it possible for me to harm them?

Chinese people have traditionally been characterized by the phrase, "When it comes to our loved ones, we wish them long life, but for people we hate, we wish them an early death." I will protect and look after something I am a part of; on the contrary, whatever I do not consider myself part of, no matter how wonderful it might be, I will not mind seeing it destroyed. For example, regardless of how unworthy my children are, I will still do my best to teach them well. No matter how dirty or ugly my pets are, they are mine and I will care for them! I am a part of them; they are a part of me. Wouldn't it be wonderful if we could be so tolerant with all things?

Therefore, we should see all humanity as our brothers and sisters. The whole universe, heaven and earth, the sun and the moon, and mountains and rivers are mine. With such wealth, what would be lacking? If we have a share in everything, there would be no more discontent. When I am a part of all there is in the world, life is indeed beautiful!

After Attaining Buddhahood

Buddhism advocates, "Buddha nature is equal for all, and everyone can become a Buddha." It is also said, "The mind is Buddha," and "A Buddha is an enlightened sentient being, and a sentient being is a Buddha yet to be enlightened." Therefore, before attaining Buddhahood, everyone is the same: a "Buddha-to-be." Once a sentient being attains Buddhahood, the spirit, life, and true mind come together completely, harmonizing with the universe, and existing with the truth. The truth is everywhere, just as Buddha nature fills the universe, appreciating the natural and peaceful Dharma joy.

After attaining Buddhahood, a Buddha's Dharma-body can continue to exist, housing the serenity of the Dharma nature. A Buddha can also dwell in the world to teach all sentient beings. For example, Sakyamuni Buddha taught in this world, showing sentient beings the benefits and joys of the Dharma. He cured them of all ills with the medicine of his teachings and spread the seeds of prajna wisdom in the mind field of all sentient beings, giving them the causes and conditions to be liberated.

The Buddha appeared as an ordinary person after attaining Buddhahood, taking the role of a bridge for all sentient beings by carrying them across the ocean of the cycle of life and death to the shore of nirvana. He rose early in the morning for the daily alms-round, taught, entered meditative concentration, contemplated, exercised, guided sentient beings with compassion, and led his sangha as the light of wisdom for the world. The Buddha was always diligent, never lax in his effort. He was of great compassion, wisdom, courage, and strength. He did not just talk emptily, but encouraged faith, understanding, and practice. He embodied compassion, loving-kindness, joy, and equanimity, and was complete in merit and wisdom. As he taught and traveled throughout the universe, he was like "the thousand moons reflected on the thousand rivers and the endless cloudless sky."

Emperor Shunzong of the Tang Dynasty once asked Chan Master Foguang Ruman, "From where did the Buddha come? After nirvana, to where did the Buddha go? Since we say the Buddha is ever-present in this world, where is the Buddha now?" The Chan Master replied, "The Buddha was born when the conditions were right and passed away when the conditions no longer existed. The Buddha came for the benefit of sentient beings and went away for their sake, too. His Dharma-body fills the universe and always resides in the un-deluded mind. As thoughts settle on non-thought, he abides in no abode. Within the pure ocean of suchness, his pristine Dharma-body exists always. The wise should contemplate as such and there is no need for any doubt."

On hearing that, Emperor Shunzong was still troubled and asked again, "Prince Siddhartha was born in a palace, but as the Buddha he attained parinirvana in the woods of the twin sala trees. He taught in the world for forty-nine years, yet he claimed he never spoke of the Dharma. The mountains, rivers, earth, sun, and moon will all come to an end. Who can be exempted from birth and death? With such doubts like these, wise one, please clarify."

Chan Master Ruman again explained, "The nature of the Buddha is beyond conditions, only we differentiate due to our delusions. The Dharma-body fills the universe and has neither arising or ceasing. With the right conditions, the Buddha appears in this world; when the right conditions pass, the Buddha enters parinirvana. He liberates sentient beings everywhere like the moon in water. Neither permanent nor impermanent; no birth and no death. Lives, yet is never born; enters nirvana, yet has not ceased. When mind sees emptiness, there is no Dharma to speak of."

The Buddha is not a deity who comes and goes without a trace. He was a living sage in history. After attaining Buddhahood, the Buddha was not a supernatural spirit but a practitioner of Humanistic Buddhism with great compassionate vows to liberate all sentient beings from suffering. The dialogue between Chan Master Foguang Ruman and Emperor Shunzong is testimony to his legacy.

Since you are also Buddha, how can you find and cultivate your Buddha nature?

At Ease through Contemplation

"We all are put at ease through contemplation; why go searching for it in some distant place?" One of Avalokitesvara Bodhisattva's titles is "at ease through contemplation," which means that if we can contemplate and reflect on ourselves, by knowing ourselves, we can be at ease.

When we contemplate others, if the self and others are viewed as one and the same, then we can also be at ease. When we contemplate circumstances, as long as we are not distracted by them, but instead are able to view them from the right perspective, then we can be at ease. When we contemplate phenomena, regardless of their myriad changes, if we just keep our needs simple, then we can be at ease. When we contemplate knowledge, which can be profound and mysterious, we can be at ease if we study it with a steady mind. When we contemplate the mind, thoughts arise in thousands of ways; if we face them with a steady mind, then we can be at ease. Ease! Ease! We look for ease everywhere we go. The fact is that when there is ease in our mind, then everything else is naturally at ease!

If we are wealthy but do not live at ease, then life is not much fun. "To have" in the world can be a source of vexation and attachments. Therefore, many cannot find ease in having money, a family, love, or high status. Because they "have," they are not at ease. For instance, politicians who have power may be stumped by difficult issues. In their search for solutions, they are not at ease. Entrepreneurs who have great wealth may be strapped for cash. In their efforts to resolve their plights, they are not at ease.

It is best if we possess fame and fortune, and at the same time, are at ease with life. But, when we are not at ease because of what we "have," then maybe we do not need to have so much since we all seek to be liberated, happy, and at ease. Look at young children. They are not at ease because of parental discipline. Married people are not at ease when their in-laws make demands of them. In different professions, when the job gets too difficult, or when there are setbacks, those on the job are not at ease.

Therefore, the true meaning of life is only successfully realized when we live at ease. Are we at ease with the right and wrong between self and others? Are we at ease when faced with fame and fortune? Are we at ease when met with birth, aging, sickness, and death? Are we at ease amidst causes and conditions and karmic retributions?

If we cannot live at ease, then regardless of the amount of wealth or enterprises we have, they only serve to burden and bind us. But, if we can remain unmoved by the "eight winds" of praise, blame, fame, defamation, profit, loss, suffering, and joy, then we are liberated. Are we not at ease through contemplation then?

Owning versus Enjoying

"Even with ten thousand acres of fertile fields, how much food could we eat in a day? Even with a thousand mansions, how much space could we use to sleep for a night?" Have we ever thought about how much we own and how much we are able to enjoy in life?

In time, even if we live to the ripe age of a hundred years, how much leisure time do we get to enjoy? The Spanish Moorish Monarch Abdul Rahman III ruled for fifty years. On seceding his reign, he lamented, "In my life, there were only fourteen days of my own that were truly leisurely and joyful!" In space, we may own a thousand grand mansions, but how many good nights of sweet slumber have we enjoyed? When it comes to people, we "possess" a family. But do the members really belong to us? We may also own many businesses, but are they reliable?

In this world, owning something does not necessarily mean that the owner enjoys it. On the other hand, not owning something does not necessarily mean that one cannot enjoy it. For instance, we may not own a skyscraper, but we can very well cool ourselves down in its shade on a hot day. The beautiful flowers in someone else's garden do not belong to us but we can always enjoy them from afar.

Someone may own a village, a town, or a city. But, we can enjoy the cool breezes and the bright moon. We can gaze at the stars. We can travel around the world. We can care about the earth. We can take all humanity as our brothers and sisters. The universe that we enjoy is so much bigger and broader than the family, village, or town anyone can own.

Someone may be a multi-billionaire. He or she can build theaters, libraries, parks, and museums. We as average citizens only make a living from our monthly salaries. But we can go watch movies and plays in the theaters, check out books from the libraries, browse the exhibits in the museums, and take leisurely strolls in the parks. We do not need to own or possess anything, yet we can have endless enjoyment!

What others own we should not be envious of, nor should we attempt to sabotage their enterprises. On the contrary, we should praise, assist, and wish them the best so that they can also enjoy our good intentions and blessings. The freeways do not belong to us, but we can cruise along on them. Neither the sky nor the airplanes belong to us, but, for a small fee, we can ride in a plane and fly through the air!

We may come into this world of ours by ourselves, then suddenly we have parents, family, teachers, friends, the community, a country, and even the entire universe in all its glory. Although we do not own any of these, we can enjoy the conveniences and benefits they render. Since we enjoy the good causes and conditions the world provides us, how can we not be grateful and wish all those who "own" our very best?

Money Is Not All-Powerful

A man made a great fortune with all his efforts. As he grew old and neared death, he stared at all the gold and treasure in his giant safe and sighed, "Oh gold and treasure, is it possible for you to save me from death?" Money may buy one many things, but it cannot buy eternal life for the physical body.

It can be said that:

Money can buy cosmetics but not elegance.

Money can buy beautiful clothes but not a beautiful physique.

Money can buy gourmet food but not a healthy appetite.

Money can buy a big wide bed but not good sleep.

Money can buy tall mansions but not high morals.

Money can buy books and magazines but not intelligence and knowledge.

Money can buy furniture and houseware but not joy and satisfaction.

Money can buy drinking buddies but not true friends.

Money can buy votes but not hearts.

Money can buy companies and banks but not wisdom.

Money can buy shouts of joy but not the show of respect with joined palms.

Money can buy high positions but not sagehood.

We have witnessed many wealthy entrepreneurs with great fortunes. When they died, the money they left behind caused terrible contention among their children. Many go to court over money, and many more become enemies because of money. So, is money good or bad? When money is used properly, it is benevolent. When it is used improperly, we can acquire unwholesome karma. As the saying goes, "Dharmas themselves are neither good nor bad, but good and bad are themselves dharmas." Similarly, money itself is neither good nor bad, but whether it brings benefit or harm depends on how we us it.

We should not be greedy for personal wealth. We should create common wealth to be shared by everyone. The sky above and the earth below, the sun and the moon, and the mountains and rivers are wealth shared by all. We should, therefore, learn from the sun and the moon and share our wealth with humanity.

Compassion, wisdom, humility, gratitude, faith, and ethics also constitute wealth. In sharing what we have, we should consider all sources of wealth those of nature, so that each kind can be fully and appropriately used.

Sickness of the Mind

Life is full of sickness. The various departments within a hospital such as pathology, neurology, osteopathy, cardiology, and gastroenterology, are evidence of life's numerous physical ailments. There are indeed a myriad of illnesses possible within the cycle of aging, sickness, and death. There are also mental sicknesses, such as greed, anger, suspicion, jealousy, delusion, and worry.

Physical sickness such as cancer, tuberculosis, and leukemia that were once considered incurable can now be treated with advanced medical treatments. However, greed, anger, and hatred, as well as sorrow and worries of the mind are more difficult to deal with.

Psychiatrists and religious leaders may be able to provide help and counseling to those with psychological problems. But, the most difficult to cure among the variety of sicknesses are self-attachment, ignorance, and delusion. These problems may confound the best of healers. Groundless fears and illusions are beyond the cure of any medical treatment available.

Consider the following joke: Once, there was a psychiatric patient who suspected that a cat was making a home inside his belly. He could not eat or sleep well because of it. The psychiatrist he was consulting tried all the methods he could employ but still could not alleviate the fears and worries of his patient. After consultation with other doctors, he decided to perform a fake operation on the patient, who was put under general anesthesia. After the "operation," as the patient regained consciousness, the doctor showed the patient a cat and said, "The cat inside you has been removed. You don't have to worry any more!" On hearing the doctor's words, the patient looked at the cat and with a worried expression told the doctor, "Oh doctor! The cat in my belly is a black one, not a white one!"

Therefore, of all the illnesses, the most difficult to cure are selfishness, clinging to attachments, and delusions. The knots we bind our hearts with are hard to untie. The hatred we harbor inside our hearts is hard to eradicate. The greed inside us is hard to put to rest. And the door to our hearts is hard to open.

In order to cure physical illnesses, we need the help of medical doctors. But for sicknesses of the mind, we have to help ourselves with the Dharma. If we want to rid ourselves of self-attachments, we need the wisdom of no-self. The *Heart Sutra* states, "In contemplating the emptiness of the five aggregates, all suffering can be alleviated." When the self and the Dharma are empty–all becomes empty, and all sicknesses can be eradicated.

The Intolerable Pain of Suffering

We all have feelings, and with feelings come pain. Within the realm of suffering, there is the suffering of pain, the suffering of deterioration, and the suffering of change. Pain itself is part of life–the pangs of hunger and cold, poverty, and anguish. Humans suffer great pain due to the five aggregates of the physical body. As for the suffering of deterioration, we suffer when our home collapses, when we are defrauded of our savings, when our reputation is ruined, and our body ages and we become ill. Then, there is the suffering of change. The world around us is not under our control. It is constantly changing due to impermanence. When faced with changes in the people around us and matters related to these fluctuations, we are often saddened by constant reminders of departed loved ones or the heartbreaking pain of lost love.

The worst source of suffering in this world comes from physical pain; if getting sick or aging is not painful, then it would not bring suffering. Since ancient times, the most inhumane kind of punishment has been the infliction of physical pain. Some parents even use corporal punishment on their children, inflicting pain to motivate them to strive harder or behave better. Some husbands hit their wives so that they will be subdued by the fear of pain. Because of physical pain, we truly know what suffering is about.

The mind and body have limits in tolerating pain; neither can endure an excessive load. Therefore, even a great hero can break down under intolerable pain and turn into a coward. In extreme pain, self-respect is hard to maintain and the meaning of life can be easily obscured! All suffering in the world comes from pain of the mind or the body. If we can train ourselves so that neither the body nor the mind will succumb to pain, then pain will no longer be a source of suffering!

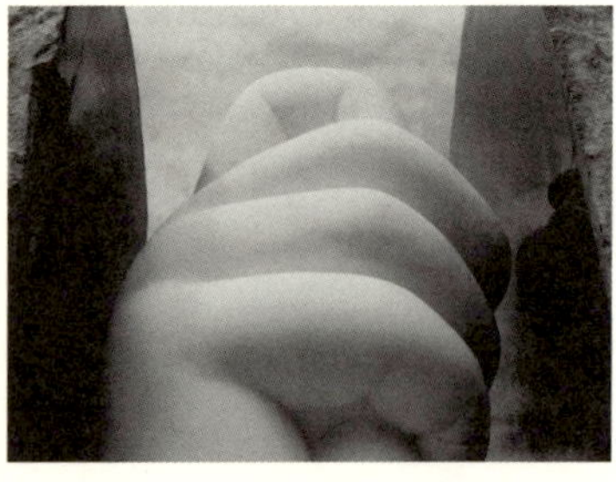

There is mental and physical suffering, as well as temporal and spatial suffering. It is also common to experience suffering that arises from people and their affairs. When the body is imprisoned or constrained, or if one is confined in a small place and the limbs are restricted in their movements–these are also forms of suffering. In enduring physical and mental suffering, sometimes we would rather die than to bear the pain. All in all, we first need to strengthen ourselves physically, and then we should fortify ourselves mentally; so that when we are faced with the pain and suffering of setbacks, we will be able to withstand them. When we no longer fear pain, the endless joy of life will be ours!

Feeling Powerless

There are many things in life that can make us feel powerless and because of this sense of powerlessness, we suffer. For instance, our children can go astray; we can fall into bad company; we can be the victims of injustice; we can be bullied; we can be cheated out of our savings; or we can have unreasonable parents and unfulfilled wishes; or we may have to face the death of our loved ones. All these inevitable sources of suffering can arouse in us a sense of powerlessness.

There are people who continually fail examinations despite their desire to progress, and the doors to further education may be closed to them. There are others who do not enjoy good health and cannot fulfill their mission in life. Moreover, some others cannot make enough money to support their families; and there are women who cannot bear children. There are also a multitude of natural and human-made disasters. All of these circumstances can make us feel powerless.

Most of us are upright and law-abiding. We are reasonable and do our best in our roles. However, there are people who are unreasonable and unjust, and we often feel powerless in dealing with them. As we get old, we also feel the impermanence of life. When we are sick, we need others to help us with our daily activities. Over time, our friends and relatives leave us one by one. Filled with worries and delusions, we have no peace of mind. All these things also make us feel powerless.

Life is indeed filled with perceptions of powerlessness! Our lovers may jilt us; our bosses may frustrate us at work. Those of us who cannot stand the heat may find ourselves trapped in the hot tropics, while those who prefer warmth may have to withstand cold climates. Whether it is human relationships, money, family, work, or stress, we cannot control it. We are powerless over so many things.

If we wish to liberate ourselves from feeling powerless in life, we must rely on ourselves. We must see through human relationships and all worldly matters. As the saying goes, "Seeing through is passing through." We should not allow ourselves to sink into the depression of powerlessness.

The shoes monastics wear have a strip of cloth sewn to the entire shoe and there are six openings symbolizing the "six perfections." These serve to remind us to look after every step, and at the same time, we should see through the impermanence of worldly matters and the illusion of human relations.

Buddhism teaches us to adapt to our circumstances. When we understand how to adapt to the circumstances we encounter and form good connections with the people we meet, we should not have to worry about feeling powerless. There is nothing in the world that cannot be resolved. If we are able to comprehend, "There is no form of the self, of others, of sentient beings, of lifespans or even of the Dharma or of non-Dharma," then there is nothing in life that we need to feel powerless over. What is there to fear?

The Malevolence of Supernatural Powers

In this world, people are always hoping for unexpected gain and advantages. Some even wish for supernatural powers so that they can know the past, present, and future. They want to see and hear in all ten directions. However, it is good that people do not have supernatural powers; otherwise, they would lead miserable lives. There are six main categories of supernatural power: the supernatural power of clairvoyance, the supernatural power of clairaudience, the supernatural power of psychic traveling, the supernatural power of mental telepathy, the supernatural power of the knowledge of past and future, and the supernatural power of ending contamination.

People should consider the potential consequences of having supernatural powers. If a tyrant had the supernatural power of clairaudience and heard his officials calling him names behind his back, he would have them killed. If couples had the supernatural power of clairvoyance and saw their partners dating others, their relationships would probably be ruined for good. Or, if a person had the supernatural power of mental telepathy and learned that friends and family members were unhappy with his or her behavior, then he or she would probably get upset, resulting in disharmony. If one had the supernatural power of psychic traveling, then one would be busy running around all day, wearing oneself out. And, if a person had the supernatural power of knowledge of past and future, and discovered that he or she had been a cat, a dog, or a bad person in the past, then he or she would not be at ease in this life. Or, if one had the supernatural power to end contamination, and therefore lived in complete non-attachment, no longer caring for family, children, fame, or fortune, would such behavior be accepted by society?

Because Buddhas and bodhisattvas have skillful means of meditative concentration, upholding the precepts, and the power of their great vows, they can utilize supernatural powers to help all sentient beings. Without these skillful means, ordinary people are much better off not having supernatural powers, as such power might be abused and cause more harm than good. Actually, it is not just Buddhas and bodhisattvas who have supernatural powers. Supernatural power permeates our universe and the dharma realms, and is present all around us in our daily lives. Is it not a miracle that one tiny seed can grow into a big tree? Is it not a miracle that a few simple words can make people laugh or cry?

There is a saying, "Strangeness arises from rarity and ceases with familiarity." If we approach life and all phenomena with a steady mind, then everything is ordinary. Therefore, if we treat space and time, and gain and loss with a steady mind, then we do not need to pursue supernatural powers. As long as we can live in peace and harmony, then our mind will be at ease.

Ryadeva, a disciple of the Buddha who possessed supernatural powers, was stabbed to death by heretics. Similarly, Maudgalyayana, another disciple of the Buddha with supernatural powers, was stoned to death. It is clear that supernatural powers cannot overcome karma and should not be the ultimate goal in one's practice.

In practicing Buddhism, we should focus on morality and compassion rather than supernatural powers. It is hoped that those who promote the use of supernatural powers will stop doing so and not become obsessed with them. Otherwise, they not only mislead others, but also harm themselves. We should advocate compassion and morality, applying Buddhist wisdom in our daily lives, so we can guide people to the right path; thus truly realizing the goal of Buddhism.

Learn to Listen

The Greek philosopher Socrates was very eloquent, and he taught people how to speak well. One day, a young man came to ask for his tutelage. The young man talked nonstop on the importance of speaking well. Socrates waited a long time for the man to finish and then asked for double the normal tuition. When asked for a reason, Socrates replied, "Well, aside from teaching you how to speak, I also have to teach you how not to speak!"

It is not easy to speak well, but it is even more difficult to listen well. Learning to listen is also an important lesson in life. In listening well, we need to pay attention and try to understand the speaker completely. It is also important to infer the full significance of what we have heard and to detect hidden meaning behind the words.

We start learning to listen when we are young–we learn to listen to our parents and to our teachers. As we enter the workforce, we have to know how to listen to different professionals, experts, our superiors, our coworkers, and the wise. In Buddhism, listening well means listening mindfully, completely, to all aspects, and with a positive mind. We need to listen completely, because we cannot take anything out of context. We must listen to all aspects, for we need to hear the voices of different sides. Listening with a positive mind means we should think positively about what we hear and give it careful consideration. We need to analyze what we hear and not jump to conclusions, which requires listening mindfully.

In listening, we should listen to what should be heard and ignore what should not be heard. We should not listen to gossip, but we must listen to the Dharma and the truth. Some people only like to listen to good news, flattery, and gossip. In reality, we should follow the principle of "hearing nothing inappropriate; speaking nothing inappropriate." Sometimes, silence is superior to sound.

Once, an air-controller asked the pilot, "What is your height and position?" The pilot replied, "I am six feet tall and sitting in the cockpit." His answer was not appropriate because he did not know how to listen.

One day, a man asked his friend to explain something to him. After much explaining, the man still could not quite get it. So his friend said, "You are really physically well-built." The man was pleased, thinking his friend had complemented him on his strong physique, not knowing that the implied message was a comment on his mental deficiency. Only those who listen well can get the hidden message.

Listening is more important than seeing. In listening, we need to pay attention to everything, not ignore others' benevolent words. We should never take the advice of others lightly. Students in class must listen attentively before they can learn well; many students get poor grades because they fail to listen well. Therefore, in the process of learning, we must first learn how to listen, for it is a major lesson in life.

The Art of Listening

When we were young, the words of our teachers never seemed to get through to our ears. When we listen to seniors talking, they always seem to be too long-winded. Even in religion, when listening to the teachings, we prefer not to understand them to the full extent. Or, when our superiors talk to us about the benefits of kindness and compassion, and the good in serving our community, we tend to regard their words as irrelevant. Sometimes while we are at work, we tend to hear without listening, and as a result, the instructions of our superiors are not carried out as expected. Even when we hear words of wisdom spoken by the virtuous and the sages, we take them as if they were of no consequence to our lives. With such an attitude, no Dharma or words of wisdom can be planted in the field of our mind, and therefore no flower of wisdom can possibly blossom there. By not paying due attention to words of wisdom, we cannot excel in the art of listening.

Other than failing to listen, refusing to listen, or simply not listening well, there are also many who only listen with a biased mind, choose to misunderstand, or only hear what they want to hear. These result in gossip and distortion, creating many problems for everyone concerned.

When listening, we should be like a water jug. The jug should not be full to the brim; if one's mind were filled with arrogance, it will be difficult for words of wisdom to enter. If the jug were contaminated, just as if the mind were imbued with prejudice and deviant views, then even the purest of Dharma water will be polluted. Or, if the jug leaks, then any sweet rain from heaven will eventually trickle out.

Listening is like planting seeds in the ground. When the land is not arable, the seeds cannot germinate. When the field is full of weeds and thorny bushes, the seedlings will not grow well. Or, if the seeds were exposed, birds will come and peck at them, leaving no chance for a harvest. Since sound is the medium for propagating the Dharma we must learn to listen!

The art of listening consists of the following four points:

1. Listen with a positive mind: Know how to listen and think posi-

tively on what is said.

2. Listen to all aspects: Because listening to one side is like remaining in the dark, while listening to all sides is needed to be objective and just.

3. Listen mindfully: Use the mind and pay full attention, also contemplate upon and remember what is said.

4. Listen completely: While listening, one should not just listen to part of what is being said, but rather to all of it, be it good or bad, positive or negative, in order to be comprehensive and not create any misunderstandings.

Kneading Dough

An asphalt road hardens after cars drive over it and press it down. Concrete is solid because of the sand and pebbles strengthening it. Steel is sturdy after being forged by fire. Dough needs to be kneaded many times before it can be made into tasty bread, noodles, or dumplings. People also need to be pressed, strengthened, forged, and kneaded in order to be of good value.

A tasty fluffy croissant and "al dente" noodles are the result of good kneading. In the army, going through training is similar to being kneaded like dough; a sterling, valiant soldier can only become so by being thoroughly "kneaded." In school, students are subject to many strict tests and examinations, big and small, to help them come through with flying colors. Likewise, farmers have no fear of inclement weather in their diligent cultivation that yields a good harvest to be shared by all. Similarly, workers may ignore personal hardships and be willing to sweat for a greater production.

Many people throughout history overcame insurmountable hardships to achieve positions in academia or to become great heroes of their times. Mahatma Gandhi, reformer and national hero of India, persevered for many years in his nonviolent resistance to any form of persecution. His tolerance for extreme hardship finally received due international attention, and India gained independence in the end. Nelson Mandela of South Africa was jailed for twenty-seven years in his fight to end apartheid in his country. His forbearance finally paid off; apartheid was abolished, and he became the first black president of South Africa. The Buddha practiced asceticism for six years with only horse oats for sustenance. After a long period of mental and physical trials and tribulations, he achieved enlightenment and became the Buddha.

There is a story about a large bell in a main shrine, which one day protested to the bronze Buddha statue, "Why is it whenever devotees come to the temple, they always bring flowers and fruit to make offerings and pay respect to you? As for me, not only do they not pay respect to me, they hit me instead." The Buddha statue replied, "Oh large bell, do you know how much chiseling, hammering, and 'kneading' I went through before I become the Buddha statue I am today for people to honor? But you can barely stand a single stroke before you wail loudly. That's why, you can only be the large bell you are today for others to strike at."

Mencius once said, "When heaven is about to bestow a task on a person, it will first test his mettle, belabor his bones and muscles, starve his body, subject him to extreme poverty, and confound his undertakings so that he learns to persevere and is later able to realize his potential in ways he could not otherwise." This means that success is only possible with "kneading."

"Without enduring bone-chilling cold, the plum blossoms will not be profuse in fragrance." Therefore, we must be like dough, able to take all sorts of kneading before we can realize our hope for success.

Half and Half

"Half and half" is a philosophy of life. In our world, half of the time is day and the other half is night. The sun and moon each takes up half of the time. Depending on which part of the world we live in, some or all of the four seasons take up half or a quarter of the limitless time.

The globe is also half and half. The Western and Eastern Hemispheres each take up half of the world, which is about half ocean and half land. Land is half hilly and half flat. Plants and animals each occupy half of the space. Society is also half and half, because openness, benevolence, and beauty only take up half while darkness and ugliness take up the other half. About half of the people are men and the other half women. Truth is only half of life and falseness the other. Even the Buddha only has half of the world, because the other half is occupied by the demons.

The same set of parents may have several children, half of whom are good children and the other half not so good. Similarly, half of the seeds sown in the fields will bloom and bear fruit while the other half wither and die. Since the beginning of time, people have wanted a complete and united world, but within the theory of "half and half," it is very difficult indeed!

There is an old Chinese saying, "Any major matter in the world will come together after a long separation and will separate after being together for a long time." There are two main ideologies in the world, democracy and autocracy, and world governments are divided half and half.

It is almost impossible for one half to rule the other half. Just as husbands want to control their wives, their wives also wish to dominate them. It is not easy for one spouse to rule the other completely. Those in power rule the average citizens while the latter have the potential to overthrow the former, because each party naturally possesses only half of the power in this world.

Water can float a boat and also overturn it. Water can put out fire while fire can evaporate water. They just take turns according to the principle of half and half: when one is active, the other waits for its time.

Therefore, while smart people despise those who are foolish, foolish people always gain at the expense of the smart ones. They each have their strengths and weaknesses.

When people can deal with "half and half" relationships effectively and accept them as a normal way of life, we can coexist in the world. If the two halves want to overcome one another, there will be a lot of fighting, and inevitably both sides will be harmed. The best we can do is to use the better and benevolent half to influence the unwholesome half, although our hopes should not be too high about how effective we can be. When people are willing to accept the better half, the worse half will naturally diminish. It is only by being able to embrace the good and tolerate the bad that we can live all-encompassing lives.

Right versus Deviant

As the saying goes, "One should rather be right and lacking than deviant and abundant." It is fundamental that our views in life be right and not deviant.

Buddhism teaches the Noble Eightfold Path for everyone to uphold. The teachings are as follows:

Right view–To have right understanding and views. Right views are the guide for cultivation, just as we need eyes to see where to go or a compass for navigating in the proper direction. Right views are also like correctly adjusting the focus and exposure on a camera to ensure bright and clear pictures.

Right thought–To have no greed, anger, or ignorance, detaching us from delusive cravings. In accomplishing this, we will be able to differentiate delusion and truth with our wisdom.

Right speech–To refrain from careless speech, slander, arrogant speech, verbal insults, and malicious, idle, or false speech.

Right action–To engage in right behavior, which means generating pure positive karma of the body, speech, and mind. Refrain from killing, stealing, and engaging in sexual misconduct.

Right living–To make a living by legal and rightful means.

Right effort–To progress vigorously and single-mindedly toward the truth, without regressing.

Right mindfulness–To uphold the Dharma with pure thoughts, without any deviation.

Right concentration–To use right meditative concentration so scattered thoughts can be centered into single-minded thinking.

The Noble Eightfold Path is guideline for everyone to uphold in life. If we do not follow the "right" path, then we will fall into the "devious" way. This is truly dangerous!

Once, a novice monk was late entering the city at night. He could not get in because the city gates were closed. So, he sat under a tree in meditation to wait for dawn. In the middle of the night, a ferocious ghost with a vicious face appeared and threatened to eat the novice monk. The latter said, "I am not your enemy, and we are far apart. Why do you want to eat me?"

The fierce ghost asked, "Why do you say we are far apart?"

The young monk replied, "I'm a Buddhist practitioner, and if you eat me, I will be reborn in the Western Pure Land. But your unwholesome deed and devious mind will only lead you to be reborn in hell. That is why we are far apart." Upon hearing this, the ferocious ghost awakened. Realizing that the devious cannot triumph over the righteous, he went away in shame.

Be it phenomena, people, or different kinds of situations, there are both those that are right and those that are deviant. We should know the difference. Therefore, it is imperative that we all cultivate our spiritual lives in order to differentiate between right and devious.

Right and Wrong Desires

Desires are generally frowned upon by major religions and some even classify the five sensual desires for wealth, beauty, fame, food, and sleep as the five roots of hell. In Buddhism, not all desires are viewed as wrong. There are positive desires as well as negative ones. For instance, the desire to learn, to lead a country and its citizens, or to seek the Dharma in order to liberate all sentient beings are considered positive desires. Without the fulfillment of these desires, life would not be complete.

Most things in the world are viewed in duality, either considered positive or negative, wholesome or unwholesome. Giving charity is an act of kindness, but if it is performed with an ulterior motive, it becomes selfish and is actually a form of taking. If we pray and chant sutras with the purpose of transferring our suffering to others, we are behaving wrongly. A life with desire in moderation for food, clothing, intimacy, and physical well-being should not be considered tainted or negative.

How one interprets a message or motivation really depends on the individual. The same words may bring joy to some and upset others. Even when the Buddha spoke the Dharma, this happened: "While the Buddha taught with one voice, individuals understood according to their own viewpoints." Because all sentient beings are different in their capacities, the Dharma they are able to accept is, therefore, not the same. For instance, if we hit someone with our fist, it is a crime. However, if we give someone a massage using the same fist, we are thanked for it. As the saying goes, "Dharmas are not good or bad in themselves, but good and bad are dharmas" This means that we should not ignore the good or the bad, because they are still guidelines we use to monitor our conduct. We can only hope that today's society reinforces wholesome and positive desires and gets rid of unwholesome and negative ones.

What are wholesome and positive desires? In our daily lives, we should be mindful of repaying with gratitude what the Buddha, our parents, teachers, and society has given us. We should be conscious of the need to help those suffering in the three lower realms of existence. We should constantly be sharing all that is good and beneficial with others.

Society should consist of workers diligently striving in their jobs, soldiers faithfully guarding the country, businesspeople honestly serving the community, teachers tirelessly educating in schools, the media objectively broadcasting the news, and artists wholeheartedly performing. Everything that improves social morals and the individual's physical and spiritual life is classified as a wholesome desire.

What are negative and unwholesome desires? Craving things that are obtained illegally or without working for them is unwholesome. Taking joy in others' failures, being jealous of others' successes, cheating, stealing, being two-faced, taking joy in hurting others, and profiting at the expense of others are all based on unwholesome and negative desires.

Life exists within the ocean of desire. The ocean of desire itself is not to be feared. Instead, we should fear sinking in it, because that would be the greatest tragedy in life.

Good Fortune versus Bad Fortune

Every person will come across both good and bad fortunes in their lives. Life is never apart from either one of them.

When we encounter either good fortune or bad circumstances, we find it almost impossible to run away from them. Everyone wants to be endowed with good fortunes and be rid of any calamities. However, both good fortune and calamity have their respective origins. Their causes are of our own creation, and we are on the receiving end of the consequences. Therefore, some find good fortune and inspiration at a snap of their fingers, while others create a catastrophe with the mere utterance of words. Some benefit from an apparent disaster, as others create an upheaval even within their own families. Some have lucky stars shining on them all the time, while others meet with sudden misfortunes.

We all wish to be lucky and stay clear of any misfortune. We all long for fortune and the absence of trouble. However, the affairs of the world are impermanent and not everything goes exactly according to our wishes. We often suffer from bad fortune more than once, but rarely do we get lucky twice. When we have troubles, they spread like wildfire and become impossible to extinguish. Therefore, we need to be aware of our own actions, cultivate merit, and create good causes and conditions. We will then be able to steer clear of potential disasters.

However, if we do encounter disaster and are confronted with property loss, death in the family, or personal suffering, we should not blame the heavens or others for our plight. Calamity and good fortune are the mirrors of causes and conditions, just as causes and conditions are the law for all good and bad fortunes. In viewing the latter, we should all realize that whatever we meet with is the result of our own doing. Whether we enjoy good fortune or suffer a mishap is often as tangled as the intricacies underlying the vexed mind versus the bodhi mind. For instance, sometimes we are faced with meritorious conditions. But because of our errant thinking, good fortune may turn out to be bad fortune. Conversely, when facing a mishap, because of our wholesome thoughts, the misfortune becomes a stroke of luck.

There is an ancient fable about an elderly man who lost one of his horses. He was very upset about the loss, but a few days later, the old horse returned with a fine stallion. In gaining a new horse after thinking he had lost the old one, the old man was very pleased with his good fortune. However, when his son rode the new horse, which he was unfamiliar with, he was thrown off and broke his back. After that, the elder considered the horse a bad omen. During this time, a war was going on, and the country was drafting new soldiers. Because the son was injured, he was exempted from serving on the battlefield, and thus survived the war. This story illustrates the saying, "In losing a horse, the old man cannot tell whether it is good or bad fortune."

We should appreciate the fact that good and bad fortunes are two sides of the same coin and are interdependent. When people excessively delight in their successes, the seeds of failure caused by arrogance are already planted. But, when we utilize compassion and righteousness in the face of a setback, adversity becomes the cause and condition for us to progress.

Laozi taught that the greatest calamity in life is discontentment. Buddhism teaches that the greatest troubles in life are the "three poisons" of greed, anger, and ignorance. There is also the saying, "Good fortune lies in not meddling in too many affairs. Calamity comes with being overly suspicious." So, if we want to stay out of harm's way and create positive causes and conditions, we should concentrate on self-cultivation. For instance, we can stay home more to reflect on our shortcomings. We can make positive connections with others. We can crave fewer material belongings. We can cultivate our compassion. We can rid ourselves of anger and hatred. As long as we have right views and right thoughts, with no selfishness or attachment to deviousness, then whether we face good or bad fortune, we will be able to gain merit and steer clear of calamity.

Sublimity and Degeneration

When a new president presides over a country, many may ask, "Is the future of the nation going to be sublime or will it degenerate?" A country needs to continually strive to improve itself in order to have a successful future; that is the way to progress. Otherwise, the country will degenerate. In order to be sublime, there should be democracy in politics, growth in the economy, harmony in society, integrity in government, and compassion and honesty in the community. The new government and its officials must embrace all of the above or the nation will degenerate.

Other than for the country as a whole, we also need to ask ourselves if we, as individuals, want to be sublime or to degenerate. In order to be sublime ourselves, we need to increase our knowledge, enhance our morals, and purify our habitual tendencies. Moreover, we need to practice compassion in action and speech, be diligent and conscientious in our work, and live simple and unpretentious lives. Otherwise, we will degenerate.

In society or in family, many strive to be sublime in every endeavor they undertake. But, others give up on themselves and refuse to change their bad habits. The only path they take is degeneration. In their quest to be sublime many struggle in adversity, wrestle with their bad habits, and grapple with their environment. They want to uplift their images, reputations, statuses, and connections with others. However, many fail to understand the intricacies of elevating one's life toward greater fame and fortune, nor do they understand the connection between self and others. They do not have the resolve to do good, nor the spirit to strive toward the path of integrity and progress. When they come across obstacles and setbacks, the only direction for them to go is down.

There is a saying: "Learning is like rowing a boat upstream. In not progressing, one will regress." This means we need to unceasingly pursue new knowledge, enhance our wisdom, and develop our thinking in order to have sublime minds. It is never easy being human. In being human, we must be compassionate, contribute, and give others joy so as to prevent ourselves from degenerating.

We have to strengthen our allegiance to our country by observing law and order. The ancients readily laid down their lives for their countries. We need to strengthen our love and care for our families, so the aged and the young are well taken care of. We must therefore be sublime in every aspect of our lives, and never allow ourselves to sink into degeneration.

Buddhism talks about ten dharma realms for all sentient beings. Above the human realm, there are Buddhas, bodhisattvas, pratyeka-buddhas, sravakas, and heavenly beings. Then there are asuras, hells, hungry ghosts, and animals below the human realm. Our conduct and cultivation are the keys to these realms. With morality, meditative concentration, and wisdom, we become sublime. With greed, hatred, and ignorance, we degenerate. Wise reader, do you want to see your life as sublime or degenerate?

Holding One's Head High or Low

In dealing with people and situations, do we hold our heads high or low? Even if it is only for our own benefit, we should be humble and lower our heads. Others will respect us for it. In our actions, we should be mindful of respecting our country and the general public, and benefiting any organization to which we belong. We accomplish these and other missions by holding our heads high but in the spirit of humility.

In Chinese history, there were many occasions in which the spirit of the wise and honorable was tested when they acted as ambassadors and diplomats for their countries. They passed with flying colors and wrote their pages in the history books with their dignified acts and wise words. However, others were not as stately, and only brought humiliation and defeat to their compatriots.

To become a noted figure in one's time, an individual must know when to advance and retreat. If we hold our heads high inappropriately, we will be viewed as arrogant. On the other hand, if we bow our heads at the wrong time, we are considered inferior. Right timing is of prime importance.

At Fo Guang Shan in Taiwan, the main entrance to the Pure Land Cave, a visualization of the Western Pure Land, is only four feet high. Any person taller than that must lower his or her head and bend forward to enter. This is to cultivate people's humility in the face of the truth. When asked how high the universe is, a Western philosopher replied, "Four feet!" Therefore, for those of us who are taller to survive in the world, we must bow our heads!

As the saying goes, "To succeed, we should be able to lower our heads; in dealing with situations, we must persevere." Many business dealings and international negotiations for conflict resolution are successful because the negotiators exercise flexibility in taking an appropriate stand.

Plants and flowers mostly grow straight and tall. However, when sunflowers ripen, they bend low. Similarly, when wheat ripens, the stalks of grain bend over. As humans, when we mature over time, we should also know when to hold our heads high and when to lower them.

When troops march in their camps, their officers require them to hold their heads high and keep their backs straight as they take long steps forward. However, once they get on the battlefield, they must stoop low and even crawl on the ground in their effort to overcome the enemy. Similarly, in everyday life, we should be humble when holding our heads high and dignified when lowering them. Then, we can follow the middle path of life without losing our dignity and the respect of others.

Between Humans and Beasts

According to Mencius, "Whoever is devoid of compassion is inhuman; whoever is devoid of shame is inhuman; whoever is devoid of courtesy and modesty is inhuman; and whoever is devoid of a sense of right and wrong is inhuman." When our behavior lacks the qualities of humanity, we will be derided as being inferior to birds and beasts.

What is the difference between humans and animals? What distinguishes us from birds and beasts? A human is considered a person because he or she has a sense of propriety and duty. A human can stand as a person because he or she possesses honesty, knowledge, and courage. A human is a person because he or she acts with humility. Accordingly, the major difference between a person and an animal is that a person has benevolence, truthfulness, appropriateness, and integrity. Therefore, to be human is to have respect for propriety and righteousness. To be human is to be grateful and have a sense of shame. To be human is to have deep affection and a strong sense of duty. To be human is to have loving-kindness and compassion.

Besides having moral integrity, a person must have ideals and aspirations. Animals only know the satisfaction of food. Horses, cattle, sheep, and deer roam the plains in search of grass and water. Tigers, leopards, jackals, and wolves prey on the weak to satisfy their hunger. Once these predators are full, a cow or a lamb will no longer arouse their appetite.

Although humans consider themselves the wisest of all creatures, there are some animal behaviors that are praiseworthy. Ants work together as a team to accomplish their goals. Lions and tigers do anything to protect their young. A dog faithfully watches through the night to provide safety for its master. A rooster crows every day at dawn to announce the arrival of morning. A carrier pigeon flies a long distance to deliver a message. Amongst birds and beasts, there are also stories of kindness and gratitude. A lamb shows filial piety toward its mother; a raven repays its parents when they get old; and a loyal dog saves its master from danger and harm. In comparison, the behaviors of some people fall below the standards for animals. It is not a complete surprise to see people who act without conscience and are ungrateful and cruel.

People have human nature and animals have animal nature. There is a definite distinction between humanly and beastly behavior. Why do people sometimes forget the fact that they are human? It is because humans also have their weaknesses. They often lose their integrity when lured with sex, money, and power. They often become irrational when engulfed by hatred and jealousy. Throughout the history of humankind, we have seen those who are willing to sacrifice their families for the sake of personal gain. We have seen brothers fight among themselves and cut each others' throats because of greed. We have also seen sons turn against their fathers for money and profit. When blinded by selfish desires, we, as humans, often lose sight of our human nature and turn into creatures of the lowest grade.

Humans should have rationality. We should have the ability to discern right from wrong, good from bad. When faced with greed and lust, we must learn to use our sense of morality to overcome our wants and desires, for fear of becoming beasts. The Buddha taught, "Every sentient being is endowed with Buddha nature." In this way, birds and beasts are no exception; they all have the same nature as humans. Therefore, being a human or an animal depends on one's ability to protect one's true nature. If we can be scrupulously honest even when there is no one around, if we can remain unmoved by carnal pleasures and substantial profits, and if we are not ashamed to face anybody or anything, we have proven ourselves to be praiseworthy as humans.

Between Deities and Buddhas

Deities and Buddhas are different and should not be confused. Deities do not necessarily have historic backgrounds. During times of superstition, humans made deities out of every natural phenomenon in the universe. For instance, there were deities in heaven, on earth, of the mountains, and of water. Then there were deities in trees, flowers, rocks, and stones, or in the various elements of thunder, lightning, wind, and rain. All in all, there was nothing in nature that did not have a god.

As civilization developed, humanity progressed from an age of superstition to one where sovereign power was supreme. In Chinese culture, many of the deities were created based on heroes of the times. Well-known personalities such as Guan Gong and Yue Fei were deities of military prowess, and Confucius, Mencius, and Zhuge Kongming became scholarly deities.

These so-called deities were none other than those who were either superior in martial arts or excelled in aiding the general public. They were personalities that members of the community yearned for. For instance, the "Old Man Under the Moon" is the modern day matchmaker, the "Disease God" is the Secretary of Health, and "Wenchang Dijun" is the Secretary of Education.

The creation of deities was the result of human misconceptions about the world of nature. Or, people might have turned to deities for assistance when encountering problems dealing with government officials. The deities were creations of their thoughts.

Some deities carried weapons, wore special garments, had beards, and even ate meat and fish. They were almost humanized. However, Buddhas are different from these deities. The Buddha was a human being. He had a birthplace, parents, cultivation, and enlightenment to the Truth. The Buddha was not a fictitious being; in fact, there is universally accepted historic proof of his existence.

The Buddha did not carry any weapon or wear any special garments. He did not reward the wholesome or punish the unwholesome. Instead, he was simply someone who gained enlightenment to the Truth and passed his wisdom on to the world, showing its people the path, giving them a direction, and leaving them his teachings. When the light of the Buddha shines in the world, we have brightness. But more importantly, we must allow the light in our hearts to shine through and to shine on others.

The Buddha is not about power. He is the Truth and a reflection of our mind. Since we each have a mind, then each of us has a Buddha in us. If we understand "the mind is the Buddha, and the Buddha is the mind," then we can look at the world through the Buddha's eyes, thereby making the world that of the Buddha. In the Buddha's world, we listen to sounds using the Buddha's ears and we speak using the Buddha's language. When we practice the compassion and wisdom of the Buddha, we become Buddhas right here and now.

Deities and Buddhas are different: not all of us can become deities, but each and every one of us possesses Buddha nature within ourselves and can become Buddhas.

The Beauty of Incompleteness

One of the most beautiful aspects of life is having a healthy and complete physical body. However, if limbs or organs were missing, or the five senses were incomplete, is "incompleteness" still beautiful?

Those who are physically challenged must not dismay! Many famous people in the world have coped with physical limitations. Thomas Edison was deaf in one ear, but he still became an inventor, bringing light to humanity. Helen Keller was both deaf and blind but she became one of the world's most inspirational people. In spite of his physical condition, Stephen Hawking has managed to become one of our era's greatest scientists. Many who lose their hearing become much more alert in their thinking, and many who lack sight develop very sharp hearing. Those who possess complete faculties may find it easy to write and paint, but it would indeed be an extraordinary achievement for those with no arms to excel in painting and calligraphy.

In the Special Olympic Games, numerous physically-challenged athletes not only overcome their physical differences, they display physical prowess through outstanding performances in different sporting events, achievements which could not be matched even by those with complete faculties. There are countless examples of people with incomplete senses living happy and healthy lives, raising families, and enjoying exceptionally successful careers.

It is not always desirable to be too beautiful or successful in our lives because we may easily become the object of others' envy. Having some missing parts may actually bring us good fortune in life. Many Buddha statues are broken in one way or another, but because they are so beautiful, they are highly sought after by world-renowned museums. A rose's thorns may be seen as shortcomings, but they act as protectors of the beautiful and fragrant flower; they are another demonstration of the value of "imperfection."

In Buddhism, the description, "Ugly monk with wonderful Dharma," comes from the idea of a monk who, although having unattractive physical features, devotes himself to practicing the Dharma. In his previous life, Venerable Master Yulin was a monastic scribe who was extremely ugly. Because of his "imperfection," he was motivated to immerse himself completely in the Dharma.

The ugly daughter of King Prasenajit in the Buddha's time chose to stay home instead of going out with her husband to social functions. As she practiced meditation in her room day in and day out, she was able to transform her appearance with her practice and became more attractive over time. On the other hand, Bhikuni Subhadra was so beautiful that she became the target of harassment by local youth. Her extraordinary beauty was a source of suffering for her. From this we can see that being too beautiful can be a handicap. As the proverb says, "The musk dies because of its fragrance, and the silkworm lives a short life due to its silk."

Visitors who tour palaces and castles often admire the dwellings of ancient monarchs and aristocrats. Though the upper class might have lived in huge luxurious mansions, they could not casually leave their homes. Their cloistered lives were not as open and broad as those of the common folks who could travel anywhere they chose.

If we learn to appreciate the beauty of incompleteness in life, then we have already achieved completeness inside ourselves.

Where Should People "Reside"?

Where should people "reside"? In homes, of course, but is home a place where we should stay forever? In the animal realm, even a little bird leaves its nest after it has grown. Or, when a puppy becomes big enough, it likes to venture out of the house to play. The Chinese character "home" is composed of a pig under a roof. If someone stays home every day with nothing better to do, how is this habit different that of a pig?

Since home is not a permanent abode, where should we "live"? Some people "settle" on money, but if they are defrauded, or their stocks plummet, and all is lost, then where will they "reside"? Others "reside" in love, for love is indeed a source of happiness in life. But, because of life's impermanence, love changes; if couples divorce and lovers become enemies, where will they "reside"? Still others "settle" themselves in high positions. However, after each election, the elected officials happily step up to their new positions as the unelected step down in dismay. After stepping down, where are they to "settle"? Still others may "reside" in their careers, but they become so busy in pursuit of success that they neglect their spouses and children. In the end, they forget they have families and even ignore their personal well-being. To counter this tendency, the *Diamond Sutra* teaches that we should not "settle" on sights, sounds, smells, tastes, feelings, or phenomena.

So where should people "reside"? "One should cultivate the bodhi mind with non-abiding." Look at the sun; it "resides" in the sky with nothing to hang onto. But it is in no danger of falling, for "non-abiding" is where it "settles." Similarly, monastics appear to be without a home, but in reality, everywhere is home for them. Their lot in life is indeed one of tranquility and liberty!

In the course of our lives, fame and fortune, money and material property are not entirely unimportant. However, we should use them and not be used by them. We should "pass through the flowering shrubs and bushes without letting a single leaf cling to us." Even Emperor Shunzhi of the Qing Dynasty longed for the tranquility and ease of the monastic life, lamenting, "A hundred years as a king is no comparison to even half a day as a monastic!"

"When we possess Dharma joy, we need not indulge in worldly pleasures." This is the best prescription for settling the mind and purifying our nature–to be able to rest our bodies and mind is the path towards fulfilled and happy lives. We should not "reside" in the five sensual desires and worldliness, but rather, live lives of simplicity and peace. We should never be slaves to money, but "settle" our mind on contentment. We can then adjust our lives accordingly, and in following our circumstances, live carefree lives!

Life Education

Although the pursuit of improving one's life has grown in importance nowadays, it seems that few people understand what it is about. Real wealth is not money, fame, or property; the most valuable thing is life itself. It is evident that our lives are infinitely more important because when we are in life-threatening situations, we will give up any amount of money in order to save ourselves.

However, our lives are not rooted in our physical bodies alone. Life needs the support of the causes and conditions provided by different members of society, without which our lives cannot be sustained. Furthermore, there is life in nature, society, and family, just as in the individual.

Life is energy, function, and action; and we need to use it to interact with one another. For instance, rain waters the woods and trees, which in turn conserve the rainwater. Animals live off the land and provide the land with nutrients in return. Life is the continual interplay of causes and conditions all around. No one can survive all by him or herself.

Those who understand life know that humans, animals, and plants all have life. Even our clothes, shoes, furniture, and dishes have life. Some people's shoes only "live" a few months, but others' "live" for a year or two. Life manifests itself through the existence and continuance of all things.

How extensive is life? It is endless! How expansive is life? It is limitless! The meaning of "Amitabha Buddha" is limitless light and endless life. It can be said that life occupies a few days, a few hours, a meal, or a breath, but it also transcends time and space!

Buddhism teaches us that "a thought embraces three thousand realms" and "all dharma realms are in the mind." Everyone embraces me, and I embrace everyone. We coexist with heaven and earth, and we live with the whole universe. There is no limit to the value of life!

There is a saying, "Mayflies are born and die within a day; human life rarely lasts more than a hundred years." However, even when the physical body has died, it is not the end of life! As we contemplate how heaven and earth endure, we can appreciate how limitless life is. The length of life is not what is most important; its meaning lies in what it creates. Advocates of life education should reflect on this!

Human Rights and Animal Rights

Civilization has progressed from the divine rights of ancient monarchies to today's democracy. In the modern era, many nations of the world are advocating human rights, especially the United States, which has protested human rights violations in China by setting many restrictions on trade with regard to granting China most-favored nation trade status and entry into the World Trade Organization. These restrictions are meant as a form of incentive to improve China's human rights record.

Many years ago in Taiwan there was an era called the period of "white terror." Human rights were not respected, and the lives of the citizens were controlled by a small number of politicians. Due to the unconscionable behavior of some officials bent on ingratiating their superiors, many people were jailed unjustly. A society without human rights inevitably throws its citizens back to an age of darkness and suffering.

Times have changed. The importance of human rights has risen in status, and the call for universal human rights echoes around the world. Dictators who were once accustomed to having their way are now restrained by public opinion. Chinese Confucianism long ago warned that, "Those who act in accord with the wish of the citizens will prosper, and those who act against it will perish." In addition, Confucianism also indicated that heaven, earth, and humans all share equal rights. Since the heavens are feared and respected by all and the earth is loved by everyone, humans should be respected universally. The same holds true today: whoever interferes with human rights is going against the times and will not be able to survive.

With human rights in place, we should now progress to respect animal rights. The Buddha said, "All sentient beings have the wisdom and virtue of the Buddha." When people randomly kill animals, they violate life like the tyrants of old. It is still injustice!

America is the most progressive country in protecting animal rights. Penalties are levied against those who carry chickens and ducks upside-down by their feet, or overload the cargo carried by animals. People who abuse their pets are often reported to state animal protection organizations. After an investigation, if they are found guilty of abuse or cruelty, they may be fined or have their pets taken away from them. In national parks, animal crossings take precedence over those of humans. In the same way, international organizations protecting animal rights are making even more advances. Heavy penalties are set for those who engage in the illegal trade of elephant tusks, rhinoceros horns, bear gallbladders, and other parts of rare animals. We should rejoice on behalf of the earth's animals!

However, there are still some developing countries where rare animals are slaughtered for their skins or other body parts. Birds are caught indiscriminately with traps, and fish are poisoned or electrocuted. In the winter, dog meat is a delicacy, while in some restaurants live fish is offered as a special dish. If such cruel acts were inflicted on the perpetrators, they would know how much suffering they are inflicting on their victims.

As Chinese proverbs say, "Do not take the lives of animals lightly; they also have skin, flesh, and bones. Do not shoot spring birds; the babies in the nest are waiting for their mother to come home."

Now that we are making advances in human rights, we hope that animal rights can also progress.

Fresh Faces of Society

Every year in July and August, there are always many graduates from colleges or other institutions joining the workforce. These tens of thousands of young graduates are the fresh faces of society.

These young people are mostly supported by their parents at home, while in school, they receive the knowledge and guidance of their teachers. They are like the children of heaven, living a carefree life, enjoying the resources of society. However, once they graduate, they have to support themselves. They may first have to linger at the threshold of various professions before they can settle on a career, and once they do, they still have to face many challenges and risks.

Young people's days are no longer as easygoing as before. Some may encounter good causes and conditions, with opportunities constantly knocking at their door, while others look everywhere but cannot find them. Therefore, these fresh faces need to use all their skills and try their utmost to find the right niche in life. Whatever job they find should be able to support them, while enabling them to accumulate experience and merit for a promotion or better opportunity in the future.

Some of these fresh faces want to fly high and make it to heaven with a single step, but heaven is way up there! Because they desire to fly too high too soon, they often fall hard back down to earth. What society has to offer at the moment may not be what they wish for. Eventually, they learn firsthand about the ups and downs of human relations. They find it difficult to handle their gains and losses and even harder to live the life they imagine for themselves. After a short struggle, they are often like plucked peacocks, helpless in their plight!

There are ten dharma realms mentioned in the *Avatamsaka Sutra*, and each of them has ten of its own dharma realms. It is like the hundreds of professions in this world. Where do the fresh faces want to end up, and can they become leaders in their fields? Since there is no free lunch in the world, success requires time and effort. Every person has the ability to start with nothing and strive for ultimate success. They can form social connections, starting with generosity and helping others, before the causes and conditions are ripe for success in the future.

Some may ask, "What does the future hold for the fresh faces of society?" The answer depends on their level of diligence, contribution, honest work, patience, good relationships with others, optimism, and progress. If these fresh faces of society also have skills, morals, perseverance, and an understanding of cause and effect, there is nothing they cannot accomplish.

These fresh faces should remind themselves of the lesson in the story of the race between the tortoise and the hare. Speed is not the key–patience is. It is not important that the flowers and leaves of their careers are always lush and beautiful; sometimes, they must be able to withstand the test of wind and rain! On the journey of life, if the fresh faces do not take advantage of opportunities when they are riding high, what will they do when spring is long gone and the cold and snow of winter have set in? When they are down and out, and job opportunities are nowhere to be found, they must have the spirit to pull themselves together and rise again. Otherwise, what hope is there for success?

People will always search for gold and diamonds buried deep in rocks and mountains, or for wild orchids blooming fragrantly on steep cliffs. So, fresh faces of society, remember that your communities will never let you down as long as you contribute. As for your future: it lies right there inside your mind! Your world and your future depend on how you choose to create them!

Intersections

There are many intersections in life. North, south, east, and west: which way shall we choose? At an intersection of life, if east is the way to kindness and west leads to evil, which way should we head? If south is ethical behavior and north is profit mongering, which way should we turn?

The *Treatise on the Awakening of Faith* says the mind has two gates; one is the gate of Buddha nature and the other is the gate of arising and ceasing. The former leads to heaven and the Buddha path, the latter to the human world and evil deeds. Where is our mind headed?

In our daily lives, we often hesitate at intersections. When we want to change jobs, we ponder whether to choose the fields of business and industry, or culture and education. An interloper may come between longtime lovers, forcing one of them to decide whether to stay or go. In an election, there is always the question of which candidate to vote for. When every choice seems like a good one, it is difficult to make the right decision. We are left wandering at the intersection, unable to decide the right way to go.

Some people have many plans for their lives. For every issue, right and wrong, gain and loss, good and bad are constantly battling for position in their mind. We are lost and drifting in the intersection without the guidance of wisdom. If we go in the wrong direction, the results can be disastrous.

Throughout the dynasties in Chinese history, some officials joined bandits rebelling against their emperor; conversely, some outlaws considered surrendering to the government. As they were at the crossroads of deciding their fate, they really needed great courage to make the decision. In addition, they also needed the wisdom to tell right from wrong, good from bad. There were numerous ministers in Chinese history renowned for their integrity and loyalty to their lords, but there were also others notorious for their treachery. Their choice to be ethical or immoral occurred only in a thought, and their choices ultimately made a profound difference in their own lives as well as in history.

Students graduating from high schools every year face the dilemma of entering college or joining the workforce. If they decide to attend college, they then have the difficulty of choosing one college among myriad options. The college-bound also have to determine which subjects to take each semester, which major to select, and which career to eventually pursue. Should those choices be based on their interests or future job opportunities? Making a choice is often difficult for anyone at any intersection.

Chan Master Danxia meant to take the imperial examination in the capital. Upon passing by a Buddhist temple, he realized that taking an examination for an official position was not as good as being tested for Buddhahood; he chose the Dharma as his way of life. There are many cases in everyday life where people checked their bearings at the last moment. They learn to turn around instead of plunging into the deep end. These are the people who did not lose their way at the intersection.

With so many intersections in life, what are our choices when we reach them? Should we choose the direction towards good or evil, morals or profit? Wise readers, you make your choice.

The Role of a Comedian

In ancient Chinese dynasties, emperors often favored ministers who would agree with anything their lords said and tried their best to keep the emperors happy in every situation. Though these ministers were not court jesters per se, they nonetheless played the role of the jester without of course the charm of one.

The "comic relief" is never the main character in a play, but he or she is not insignificant either, making others laugh and bringing them joy. Unlike the court jester who pleases only the emperor, the comic relief brings laughter to thousands. In a play, there are those who are loyal and righteous and those who are wicked and vicious. To play the role of a righteous hero, one needs integrity; and to play the role of a crook, one needs the look of a traitor. Each of these roles has a measure of good and evil, but the comic relief has neither. As such, it is not an easy role to play.

Most people enjoy watching clowns, mainly to see how well they "clown" around. There are different types of clowns: those who are good make people laugh with every gesture; those who are not merely put on an act and make fun of others. Life is also a stage; if we cannot play the role of the righteous hero, we should at least play the part of the clown. However, we should never play the crook.

Do you want to be a clown? Consider the following verse:

Amidst the applause and cheers,
tears are brimming behind the smiles;
Bringing joy when the curtain rises,
and left with loneliness as the curtain falls.
To be able to stand here on stage has involved so many trials,
and so many tears.
The pain of failure and the encouragement of success,

Who knows how long this cycle has gone on?
Clown, oh clown! You change your bitterness
into delight for all to enjoy!

Every play needs a comedian. In real life, we may be neither great nor noble, but we can always play the role of a comedian well enough to bring happiness to others!

Life Is But a Dream

Life is like leaves floating on water, as fleeting as a dream! In Buddhism, the six human consciousnesses are consciousnesses of the eyes, ears, nose, tongue, body, and mind. When our eyes, ears, nose, tongue, and body are sleeping, our mind may remain "awake" via dreams. Even though dreams are not real, they may seem real. We can travel the world and meet many people through our dreams.

In real life, some people enjoy dreams because they can "add" many years to life. In a dream, some people live through decades or even a life of fame and fortune. On the other hand, many people fear dreams because they may have nightmares, and wake up in a cold sweat of terror!

Buddhist sutras provide many reasons for dreams. They may merely result from poor health, poor memory, delusions, and waking thoughts. On the other hand, some believe that their dreams forecast what will happen in the future.

In reality, life is like a dream. Within this dreamlike life, we have further dreams. Therefore, ancients often reminded us that we are "mad people talking in our dreams."

As the saying goes, "The six realms clearly exist in dreams. But upon waking, we find them all empty." Therefore, the wise say, "I know that life is but a dream from which I should awaken." In life, dreams trouble us persistently.

There are many kinds of dreams. Some people dream about being beaten and murdered or even dismembered; those are, of course, nightmares. Some dream of visiting strange places and seeing curious things and beings; theirs are strange dreams. Others think about what they have learned while dreaming; these are dreams of wisdom. There are also times when we dream of what we have not known, seen, planned, or thought of. Various kinds of dreams can bring us happiness, terror, gain or loss.

Dreams are only a phenomenon of our consciousness. We all dream, and we sometimes hope that all of our dreams will come true. However, this is not a good idea. If all our dreams–include dreams of sorrow, unresolved difficulties, struggles for survival, or unfulfilled cravings–came true, how could we withstand them?

We should transform our positive dreams into goals for life. Our goals should be career success, a bright future, the acquisition of wisdom, and the development of our morals. When our goals are realized, then a life based on dreams will become a life based on reality.

To Be at Peace with Living and Dying

Talking about death has always been taboo. But, with the changing times, this has become a very popular subject. In fact, life's two major questions are about "living" and "dying."

Living requires a place to sojourn; dying requires a place to go. Some find it hard to create a place to live; others worry about where they will go when they die. The study of Buddhism is actually the study of living and dying. For instance, Avalokitesvera Bodhisattva relieves suffering, resolving the problems of living. Amitabha Buddha accepts sentient beings into the Western Pure Land, resolving the problems of dying. But when we change into a new body, we cannot recall our previous lives. Therefore, we do not understand the relationship between living and dying–the most difficult problem in life.

There is a day when we are born and there will be a day when we die. After death, we will be reborn. Birth and death, living and dying, have no beginning and no end. Like the hands of a clock going around the face over and over, or the never-ending rim of a round bowl, birth and death are a cycle. When we plant a melon seed, we get melons; when we plant a bean, we harvest beans. Yet, because the cycle continues, planting is not the beginning, and harvesting is not the end: there is an end in the beginning, and a beginning in the end.

In Buddhism, many highly-cultivated monastics reflect with joy on living and dying. They believe that we should come into this world joyfully and leave it likewise, knowing that there is no end to all the comings and goings! Throughout history, some Chan practitioners passed away while farming the land; some held their own funeral services before dying; others played the flute and left sailing on a boat; still others journeyed east and west bidding farewell to friends and relatives before dying. As they come for the sake of sentient beings and go for the same reason, they have no attachments with either coming or going. Old clothes need to be replaced with new ones; we need to move to a new house when the old one is no longer habitable. Old cars are phased out over time and replaced with new models. So when the physical body ages, why should we not change to a new one?

Francois Rabelais once said, "I am going to seek a great purpose, draw the curtain, the farce is played." He was completely at ease and without any attachments when faced with death. On his deathbed, Jean-Jacques Rousseau comforted his wife, "Don't be sad! Look at the bright sky on the other side. That is where I'm going!" This is an indication of a carefree life.

Death is not to be feared; dying is simply migrating. When we move to another country, we must have sufficient resources to live there. As long as we have merit and the wealth of the Dharma, we need not fear the prospect of living in a new land. Euthanasia has become an increasingly visible phenomenon. To die painlessly is of course much better than to die in pain. If we have lived a happy life, we naturally fear a painful death. But if living and dying are one and the same, why fear death and cling to life?

The Pure Land School of Buddhism considers death to be rebirth. To be reborn is like going abroad, or moving to a new house. So, dying is something to be happy about. It is simply the turning point between two phases, the beginning of life in another form. Therefore, there is no need to be afraid. When death arrives, we should take it as it comes and accept it peacefully!

High, Medium, and Low Grades

People can be ranked into high, medium, and low grades, just as we do with the things we use and the food we eat. Teachers in school regularly assess their students this way, and, in the army, officers are ranked in a similar manner. A brigadier general is given one star, a major general two, a lieutenant general three, and so on.

We can evaluate things in the world the way we rate hotels: five-star, four-star, three-star, and some which may not even be worthy of a one-star rating. For historic sites, there are also first, second, and third class ratings. It is natural that things in the world be divided into so many grades. Even members in a family are classed by generations of grandparents, parents, and children. That is the natural filial order.

Our behavior can also place us in a hierarchy of grades. When we have morals, knowledge, and abilities, and when we work for the benefit of the community, we are in the premier grade. When we merely do our jobs well and put forth our best efforts, we are in the middle. But if we are bent on taking advantage of others, our unethical behavior and crooked ways will place us in the lowest grade. Therefore, we should constantly remind ourselves to behave in a manner appropriate to the grade we want to be in.

In speaking, as well, there is high-grade speech, which is elegant, respectful, and full of praise for others. Next there is medium-grade speech, which should be correct, and appropriate to our position in society. Low-grade speech is unsuitable and harsh. Similarly, in writing, high-grade writers are thorough and concise, or descriptive and lively. The medium ones are clear and straightforward, with no special flair. And the low-grade writers are boring and without substance. In both speaking and writing, we need to keep in mind which grade we want to belong to.

In Buddhism, when we talk about repentance, taking initiative, and making vows, there are also three grades. In high-grade repentance, we bleed through our pores. In medium-grade repentance, we perspire in our fervor. And, in low-grade repentance, we shed hot tears of remorse.

In life, even if we cannot be a high-grade person, and act and speak as such, we should at least not fall into the low grade. By being in the middle, we will not damage the reputation of our community, nor harm others with our behavior, but instead conduct ourselves in a manner appropriate to who we are. We should approach life and its tasks with a steady mind and simply be ordinary people. Then, at least we can be at peace with life.

The Importance of Harmony

Harmony between people is very important. In social interactions, harmony results from friendliness and love, mutual benefits, shared ambitions, or simply being from the same school, region, or social group. But in reality, wherever there are people, there are bound to be differences and conflicts of interest, and harmony is not always easy to achieve.

In today's society, many conflicts arise because of disagreements regarding ideals and viewpoints, causing distinctions between individuals, parties, and organizations. In addition, many people are intolerant of others because of differences in religion, national or ethnic origin, language, and cultural practice. So how can a nation achieve harmony among its citizens?

In Buddhism, there is a saying, "A monastery prospers when there is no issue to dispute." There is no "issue to dispute" only when people are in harmony. One way the members of a sangha attain harmony between people and their affairs is by adhering to the "six points of reverent harmony"–to reside in harmony, to speak in agreement, to share in joy, to uphold the same precepts, to hold the same views, and to share the same benefits. The "seven methods of settling arguments" according to the *Vinaya* is also an example of how harmony is achieved in a sangha.

The *Amitabha Sutra* says, "In the Western Pure Land of Ultimate Bliss, all the excellent beings assemble together in one place." That is a manifestation of harmony. Harmony creates a pure land: a family in harmony means happiness for the family; a community in harmony spells peace for the community. Harmony will be achieved only if we have tolerance and respect for others. When we realize there will always be differences between individuals, we will be able to accept and tolerate these differences. Just as a pond of white lotus flowers looks particularly beautiful with green leaves as a backdrop, or butterflies flitting about in the garden look especially pretty with their multicolored wings, everything looks more beautiful when the differences are embraced. Rainbows, too, are dazzling because they embrace different colors of the spectrum, displaying them in perfect harmony.

As communal creatures, human beings need the help of others to survive. Helping others enables us to share in the achievements of the group. We must learn, then, to appreciate the value of harmony. In a family, there must be harmony between spouses, siblings, parents, and children; in an organization, harmony must exist between partners, coworkers, employers, and employees. As the Chinese saying goes, "A harmonious family brings prosperity, for harmony breeds good fortune." Or, "When two people share the same will, they can overcome all obstacles." This should help us realize just how important harmony is!

Colors of the Rainbow

Is any single color the one most beautiful color in the world? Red, yellow, blue, green, white, black, and purple are all candidates, but only when they come together in a rainbow do they display their true beauty.

Early movies were silent and in black and white, but today we can enjoy full-colored animation and live-action films. Printing started with black and white prints and expanded to the present computerized color publications. Modern people dress in many styles, in a wide variety of colors and materials. We also prefer food to be colorful as well as delicious and aromatic.

White clouds in the sky may look prettier than dark ones, but they cannot compare to rainbows and sunsets, which paint the canvas of nature with exquisite colors. Hikers are charmed by the singing and chirping of birds in the woods, and divers are attracted by beautiful fish in the sea. People love spring because of its vibrant blossoms, and even babies prefer to look at colorful objects.

There are some people whose speech is as beautiful as poetry or painting. Their wonderful articulation is vibrant with life and color. Likewise, some people can write skillfully. They fill their stories with colorful emotions and feelings, captivating their readers with every twist and turn.

We all want to live an active life that is as colorful as a rainbow. But some people live regretful, gray lives. Others see their lives as gloomy, because they lack good health, youth, ideals, goals, joy, and friends. So how do we live a life of wonderful colors? We need to create it ourselves by contributing to community, making connections with others, radiating joy, and responding to our circumstances. When we are welcomed by others, and are at ease everywhere we go, with smiles and praise, we can create and live colorful and active lives.

Whenever we apply colors, we know that just using one is monotonous. Similarly, we should not just do one thing all the time. We should be like Avalokitesvara Bodhisattva and take up many roles. At home, we need to play well our roles as wives, husbands, children, parents, or in-laws. At work, we have to know our roles well, too. Supervisors should care for their subordinates, who in turn should be supportive and responsible to their supervisors. Teachers should be tireless in their role as educators, and city workers should be dedicated to serving the public.

If we can share our kindness and love with the world, offer our pure hearts in all the ten directions, and make connections with others through our benevolence, we can paint the world with beautiful colors. Then, naturally, we can live an active life celebrating the colors of the rainbow.

Notes

Notes

Notes

Notes

Notes

Notes

Notes